FLORA HIBERNICA

The wild flowers, plants and trees of Ireland

FLORA HIBERNICA

The wild flowers, plants and trees of Ireland

JONATHAN PILCHER
AND
VALERIE HALL

The Collins Press

Published, 2001 by The Collins Press,
West Link Park, Doughcloyne, Wilton, Cork, Cork
Reprinted 2001

© Text Jonathan Pilcher and Valerie Hall
© Photographs Jonathan Pilcher with contributions by Valerie Hall
and Robin Govier

Printed in Spain by Estudios Gráficos Zure, S.A. – Bilbao
Graphic Designer: Jackie Raftery

This publication has received support from the Heritage Council
under the 2001 Publications Grant Scheme.

ISBN: 1-903464-03-X

CONTENTS

Preface

This book has been produced in response to requests from Irish wild plant enthusiasts who wanted to understand more about the origins and present diversity of Ireland's botanical landscape. We were often asked at a Field Club or Historical Society and by our own students if there was an illustrated book for the non-specialist which would describe Ireland's botany and detail its history and development. Our response was that such information had been covered in the masterful works of the great Irish botanist, Robert Lloyd Praeger, but that there was no single illustrated text written with the non-specialist in mind. Over the years, conversations held with non-specialists convinced us that there was a demand for a book illustrated with photographs which would describe the major Irish ecosystems as they are today and as they have developed over approximately the last 10,000 years, since the end of the last glaciation.

Most of the texts available to the non-specialist are based on observations from Great Britain. This book aims to describe the Irish dimension of the botany of these islands. Ireland and Great Britain have many species in common but, overall, Ireland's flowering plant flora is a much reduced version of that of Great Britain, with some redress coming from a small group of plants which are unique to Ireland. Ireland is not merely a botanical 'poor relative' of the larger island with its greater range of habitats. Ireland's extreme westerly position on the coast of Europe imparts a much damper and milder climate which, in turn, influences species distribution and manner or place of growth.

The book is based on our personal research and experience and we hope it will heighten awareness and interest in the flowering plants of a relatively small area of Europe which has such great landscape and botanical diversity.

JONATHAN PILCHER
VALERIE HALL
OCTOBER 2001

Acknowledgements

Great gratitude is due to Dr Robin Govier. For over 30 years he has been our friend and colleague and we acknowledge with sincere thanks the great contribution he has made to Irish botanical studies through a lifetime of service to students who have studied at Queen's University Belfast and as Editor of *The Irish Naturalists' Journal*. We are indebted to Peggy, Vincent and Dr Siobhan Geraghty for their wonderful hospitality, and for bringing us to see places and plants in Counties Tipperary and Clare. Even the worst of the winter sleet did not deter their best efforts.

To Maura Scannell, Ralph Forbes, Paul Hackney and Catherine Tyrie who have been clear and steady beacons. To Associate Professor David Lowe of the Department of Earth Sciences, University of Waikato, Hamilton, New Zealand for valuable discussions on early drafts of the text and to Drs Matt McGlone and Janet Wilmshurst of Landcare, New Zealand for their encouragement. To George Hall for meticulous attention to reading final drafts of chapters. To Jackie for her imaginative use of colour and design. The errors are entirely our own responsibility.

Note on plant names

We have followed both the Latin and English nomenclature of the *Flora of the British Isles* by Clapham, Tutin and Moore (1987). The Latin nomenclature of the European flora has been in flux during the last twenty years as modern taxonomic methods involving chemical and particularly DNA analysis shed new light on plant relationships.

We apologise to Irish language readers for the absence of Irish plant names. We believe it would be foolish for non-Irish-speaking authors to attempt to include Irish names. These may be obtained from the *Census Catalogue of Ireland* and from *An Irish Flora* by Webb, Parnell, and Doogue, (1996).

Timescale for Ireland's vegetation since the last glaciation

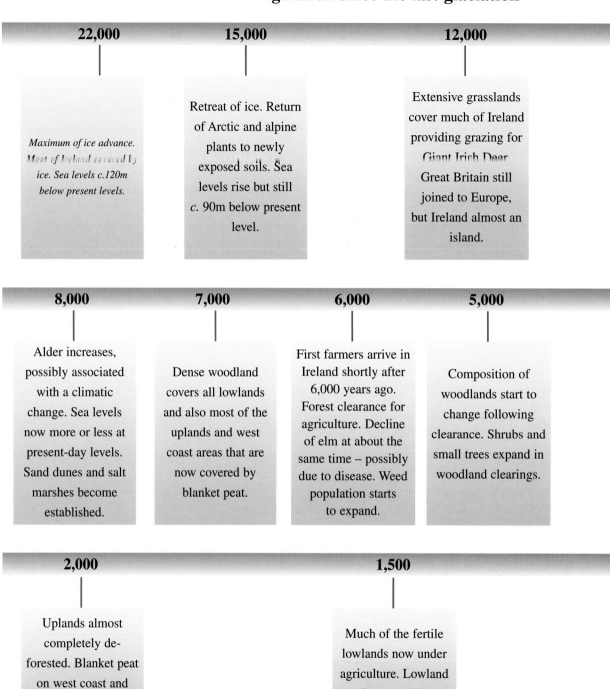

22,000

Maximum of ice advance. Most of Ireland covered by ice. Sea levels c.120m below present levels.

15,000

Retreat of ice. Return of Arctic and alpine plants to newly exposed soils. Sea levels rise but still *c.* 90m below present level.

12,000

Extensive grasslands cover much of Ireland providing grazing for Giant Irish Deer. Great Britain still joined to Europe, but Ireland almost an island.

8,000

Alder increases, possibly associated with a climatic change. Sea levels now more or less at present-day levels. Sand dunes and salt marshes become established.

7,000

Dense woodland covers all lowlands and also most of the uplands and west coast areas that are now covered by blanket peat.

6,000

First farmers arrive in Ireland shortly after 6,000 years ago. Forest clearance for agriculture. Decline of elm at about the same time – possibly due to disease. Weed population starts to expand.

5,000

Composition of woodlands start to change following clearance. Shrubs and small trees expand in woodland clearings.

2,000

Uplands almost completely de-forested. Blanket peat on west coast and uplands well established.

1,500

Much of the fertile lowlands now under agriculture. Lowland bogs at their maximum extent.

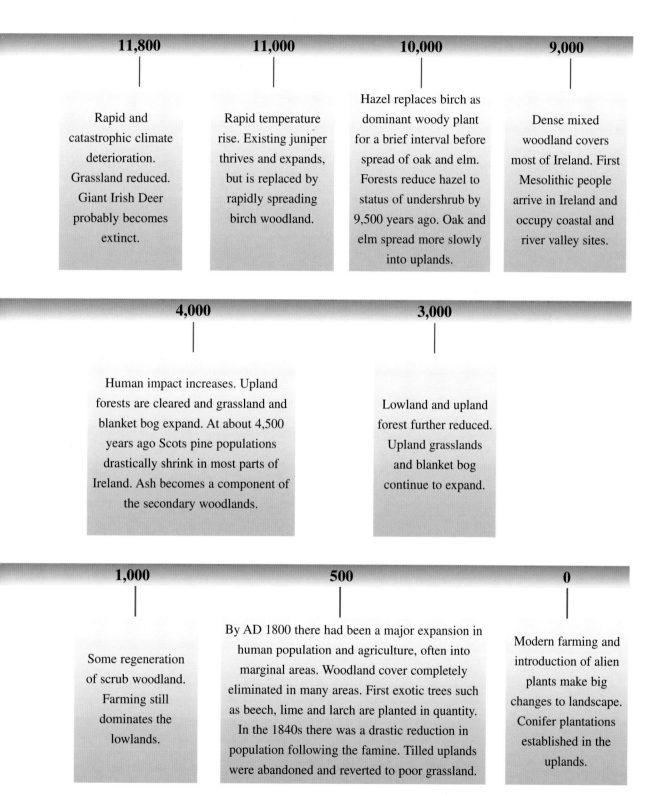

11,800

Rapid and catastrophic climate deterioration. Grassland reduced. Giant Irish Deer probably becomes extinct.

11,000

Rapid temperature rise. Existing juniper thrives and expands, but is replaced by rapidly spreading birch woodland.

10,000

Hazel replaces birch as dominant woody plant for a brief interval before spread of oak and elm. Forests reduce hazel to status of undershrub by 9,500 years ago. Oak and elm spread more slowly into uplands.

9,000

Dense mixed woodland covers most of Ireland. First Mesolithic people arrive in Ireland and occupy coastal and river valley sites.

4,000

Human impact increases. Upland forests are cleared and grassland and blanket bog expand. At about 4,500 years ago Scots pine populations drastically shrink in most parts of Ireland. Ash becomes a component of the secondary woodlands.

3,000

Lowland and upland forest further reduced. Upland grasslands and blanket bog continue to expand.

1,000

Some regeneration of scrub woodland. Farming still dominates the lowlands.

500

By AD 1800 there had been a major expansion in human population and agriculture, often into marginal areas. Woodland cover completely eliminated in many areas. First exotic trees such as beech, lime and larch are planted in quantity. In the 1840s there was a drastic reduction in population following the famine. Tilled uplands were abandoned and reverted to poor grassland.

0

Modern farming and introduction of alien plants make big changes to landscape. Conifer plantations established in the uplands.

The timescale is in years before present, based on calibrated radiocarbon dates, tree-ring dating and historical information.

Margin of the ice sheet in Greenland – Ireland as it might have looked as the glacial ice retreated. (Photo: V. Hall.)

Present day aerial view of Ireland some 14,000 years later. What has happened in between?

1 INTRODUCTION

As seen from the air or from space Ireland is a green island. What are the types of plant and where do they grow, that make the many shades of green? While Ireland shares much of its flowering plant flora with Great Britain, there are distinct differences. Ireland is more westerly and oceanic than Great Britain causing some plants to inhabit different situations than in Great Britain. For historical reasons there are also fewer flowering plants here – there are some 2,200 flowering plants in France, 1,128 in Great Britain and only 815 in Ireland. There are, however, about fifteen plants in Ireland that are not found in Great Britain.

Climate and landscape

While soils and local factors always have a part to play in plant distribution, it is Ireland's climate that is the major controlling factor on the range of plants that grow here. The mild Irish climate rarely gets cold enough for the temperature to drop more than a few degrees below freezing, and more than a few consecutive days of sunshine or a few weeks without rain are similarly rare.

Our climate is so mild because it is influenced by the ocean that surrounds us, with the flow of warm water from the Gulf Stream, which crosses the Atlantic from the Gulf of Mexico, sweeping along Ireland's shores. The ameliorating effect of this constant stream of warmth is most clearly seen when we look at other coastal areas of the globe at the same latitude but which are not bathed in heated water. On the other side of the Atlantic in Canada the Hudson River and

Hudson Bay freeze for three months of the year. Whereas the average July temperature is +10 to +20°C on both sides of the Atlantic, the average January

Grey soils and sparse vegetation covering a deglaciated landscape in Greenland provide an image for Ireland 14,000 years ago. (Photo: V. Hall.)

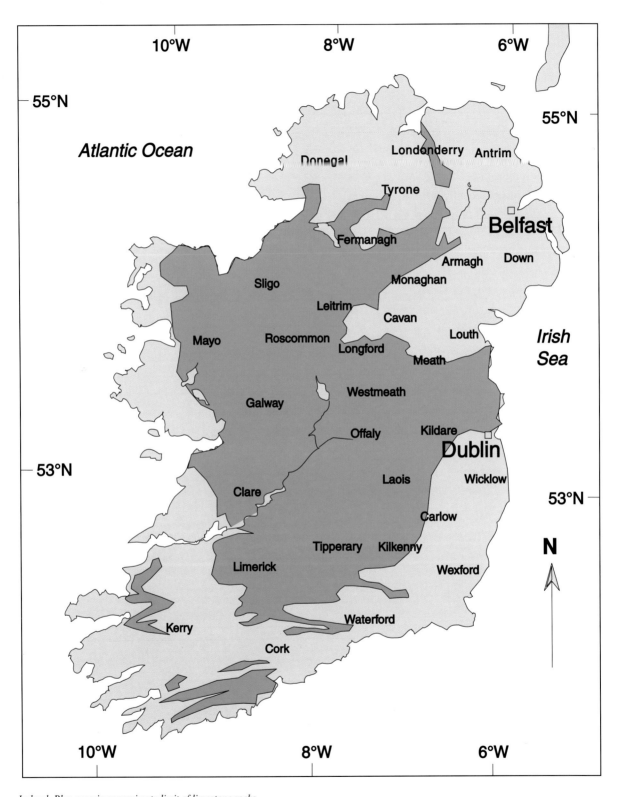

Ireland. Blue area is approximate limit of limestone rocks.

temperature in Hudson Bay is -20 to-30°C, in contrast to Ireland at +5 to +10°C.

The mild Irish climate, together with complex and varied soils, has led to a surprisingly diverse flora for such a small island, including plants from the Arctic and the Mediterranean.

We were reminded of the special oceanic Irish climate recently when a visiting colleague from Poland was very excited to see ivy *(Hedera helix)* growing commonly on walls and trees. Ivy does well in the mild climate of Ireland where it grows and flowers prolifically, but in our colleague's home near Krakow it is a rare, protected plant at the most easterly limit of its distribution, just about tolerating the extremes of the cold and dry continental climate and perhaps not surviving in harsh winters. In Ireland some plants like the bright blue-flowered spring gentian *(Gentiana verna)* grow only in the mild and damp west, in particular on the famous limestone pavement of the Burren in County Clare. Other plants which thrive in mild

conditions are common throughout the country. The tall purple-flowered foxglove *(Digitalis purpurea)* often with its visiting bees, and spiny-leaved whin *(Ulex europaeus)*, with its fragrant yellow flowers, add vivid colour to the cool clear blues and greens of an Irish spring morning. All these plants grow where the climate is damp, mild and relatively frost-free.

The end of the last glaciation
To understand the present flora of Ireland we need to go back to a time 20,000 years ago, to an Ireland which was barely visible as most of it was covered by a huge sheet of ice. This ice blanket

Rockrose and gentian, characteristic alpine plants, have survived in Ireland from times before forests covered the island.

The rounded islands of Strangford Lough are drumlins left behind by the retreating ice sheets.

The gravel ridge in the background is an esker, formed as the bed of a river flowing under the ice sheets of the last ice age. Eskers have been extensively quarried for their gravel.

was not a thin coating, but could have been up to 1km thick in some places and covered all of Ireland south to about the line joining Wicklow and Limerick. Even beyond the southern limit of the ice, little grew in the harsh treeless conditions.

From the point of view of the history of Irish plants, the end of the last glaciation is a convenient starting point as the landscape then was a 'clean slate' almost devoid of plants. Of course, there were plants here before the last glaciation, in fact over the last two million years there have been a number of glaciations with warm intervals or 'interglacials' between, each with its distinctive flora. Each of these assemblages of plants was cleared away by the ice of the next glacial advance. Thus, when we talk of 'native plants' we

do not mean they are plants that have always been in Ireland, because 20,000 years ago there were no plants in most of Ireland. By native plants we mean only those plants that arrived since the great melt at the end of the last glaciation 15,000 years ago, but before the arrival of the first people about 7,000 BC.

The retreat of the ice

As the ice retreated from Ireland, the new landscape, re-modelled by the ice, was revealed. The melting ice uncovered the small rounded hills or drumlins of boulder clay, moulded by the pressure of the ice, that form the characteristic 'basket of eggs' landscape of counties Mayo, Down and Armagh. At the same time, rivers flowed under the ice taking melt-water to the ice sheet margin.

These rivers built up layers of sand and gravel that now form ridges or 'eskers' across the countryside like winding railway embankments, much evident in the Irish midlands.

To try to envisage the conditions in which plants first colonised Ireland we have to look in the modern tundra. We will never find modern parallels to the new ice-free Ireland as these habitats belong to the past. The mountains of central Norway or remote areas such as the Lofoten Islands off the Norwegian coast provide us with some illustrations of what Ireland may have looked like in those ancient times. Today, Ireland is famous for a landscape dominated by all shades of green which vary in hue and intensity with the seasons; even in winter's depths the landscape is always verdant. In contrast, winters at the end of the last glaciation were still cold enough to permit little plant cover.

New topsoils were mostly grey or beige with thin coverings of vegetation in spring and summer. The land was colonised first by algae, lichens and mosses which could withstand the extremes of light and variations of temperature throughout the year. As summer progressed the fruiting bodies of the small ground-hugging plants added specks of orange, yellow and red to the green of the leaves. Slowly the pale topsoils darkened as the dead plants decomposed and added the first humus to the soils, thus preparing them for the next wave of colonising plants.

At the same time, the water of the many pools and lakes became green with algae, some of which were brought in on the bodies and feet of the first of the newly-returned migratory birds. The water was rich with nutrients washed out from rocks ground by the glaciers and churned by the waters of the melting ice.

Juniper is a hardy arctic plant and the first woody shrub to colonise the newly deglaciated landscape. The blue berries are in fact small one to six-seeded cones. The cones are one of the 'botanicals' used to flavour gin.

The cloudberry, with starry white flowers and orange berries, is a common tundra plant (here photographed in Norway). It grew in Ireland at the end of the last glaciation and a few plants still remain in the Sperrin Mountains today.

The brown muds found at the bottom of many lake sediments, made up of the dead remains of the algae that flourished in those first post-glacial summers, also contain the fossilized pollen and spores that allow us to discover the story of the first plants to bring green life back to Ireland.

As the new topsoils were exposed to light and warmth for the first time in millennia, the more advanced conifers and flowering plants also swiftly returned. Those cold-tolerant plants, which survived in the tundra lands to the south of the ice, were the first to expand northwards. Only a few species could survive the great fluctuations in temperature which prevailed in Ireland as it was released from the ice. Shrubby juniper (*Juniperus communis*), dwarf birch (*Betula nana*) and dwarf willow (*Salix herbacea*) along with leafy saxifrages (*Saxifraga* species), docks (*Rumex* species) and mugwort (*Artemisia vulgaris*) grew and flowered during the first warm summers. The dark

The cloudberry is common enough in Norway to be used as a yoghurt flavouring!

green of the junipers, the silver-green of the mugwort leaves and the reddish leaves of the dock were joined by the white, yellow and rosy-purple flowers of small saxifrages to form a dense covering to the soils.

One of the most characteristic plants of tundra regions now, as then, is the juniper. In tundra regions this low-growing, woody conifer has stems which sprawl several metres along the ground. Where the branches touch the ground at intervals they can root, causing the shrub to form a woody thicket less than one metre tall. Today, juniper is widespread in the high latitude and high altitude regions of the Northern hemisphere but is uncommon in Ireland. It may be found only in rocky places in the west and north, in mountain ranges and also in

Many of the first Arctic colonisers of the Irish landscape now survive only in places when dense forest never grew, such as these mountain tops.

Dwarf willow.

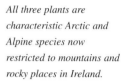

All three plants are characteristic Arctic and Alpine species now restricted to mountains and rocky places in Ireland.

Club-moss (above).

Crowberry (below).

some exposed coastal and cliff situations, particularly on limestone-derived soils, where it grows close to the ground. It is also seen in a larger and more upright form in some lowland limestone areas.

In many parts of Ireland the landscape must have appeared, yet again, snow-covered for a few weeks each summer as the mountain avens (*Dryas octopetala*) covered the land with its bright, white blossoms, followed by pale silky seed-heads. Today, this plant is common in Iceland but is rare in Ireland, restricted to limestone areas and upland

Mugwort, a tough tundra plant now a common weed of cultivated ground.

sites including some in the counties bordering the western coast. Eleven thousand years ago it was so common throughout many parts of north-west

Europe that its Latin genus name has been given to the last short cold period before the start of the present interglacial, hence that time is called the Younger Dryas Period (approximately spanning the period 12,300 to 11,500 years ago). Its fossilized pollen grains have been found in the sediments which first formed in those summers at the end of the last glaciation when conditions were still very harsh. Frequent finds of fossil mugwort pollen show that it also tolerated the harsh conditions at this time.

Common today in Scandinavia with the mountain avens is the cloudberry (*Rubus chamaemorus*). It is now very rare in Ireland but sufficiently common in Norway to be used in commercial fruit yoghurts! The shrub looks like a low-growing version of a raspberry but with orange fruit. We know from the ancient fossil pollen record that it was quite abundant in Ireland at the end of the last glaciation. A few plants were still present in the Sperrin Mountains in County Tyrone recently.

The summit of Slieve Donard, the highest peak in the Mourne Mountains in County Down, is one of the sites where there are three further Arctic survivors. The ice here was thick enough to cover these high mountains and the smooth top of the peak was polished by the sliding, melting ice. The Arctic plants would have been among the first to colonise the mountain after the ice retreated. In spite of thousands of visitors walking over the top of Slieve Donard and picnicking on it, there are plants of the tundra: dwarf willow, the crowberry (*Empetrum nigrum*) and alpine club moss (*Diphasiastrum alpinum*). It is sobering to admired the plant, we could not help wondering whether this same colony had been there for over 10,000 years. In the lowlands, on the walls of the great

This view over Correl Glen National Nature Reserve in County Fermanagh is probably representative of the mid post-glacial forest canopy.

realise that these species have been on top of Slieve Donard for longer than people have been in Ireland.

Saxifrages are common in Arctic regions but have a few species surviving in Ireland. The authors were walking in the Fermanagh hills recently and sat down to rest on a summit where there was a rocky outcrop and at the very top of this was a large colony of mossy saxifrage (*Saxifraga hypnoides*). As we

Clonmacnoise monastery there grow many plants of the rue-leaved saxifrage (*Saxifraga tridactylites*), another survivor that has found a place where there is high light intensity and freedom from competition and shade. If you want to meet the real pioneers, put on your climbing boots and search the mountain tops, cliffs or inaccessible places, unless that is, you will settle for the dock which, although a very common weed of waste

The strawberry tree is one of a small group of plants native to Ireland but not to Great Britain. Its home range is from the Mediterranean to Brittany.

places (see Chapter 8) is, nonetheless, a survivor from the tough times in the past.

Today, Scotland and the high English Lake District have many more of the tundra survivors than there are in Ireland. How is it that plants that survived the harsh conditions of the last glaciation are not more common today? Although they cope well with cold, they are not adapted to life under shade. In the early post-glacial times these plants were abundant throughout Ireland, but when the forest trees arrived, they were shaded out from all but the most exposed places where the trees could not grow or where tree cover was thin. In Ireland even the now-treeless slopes of some of the high mountains were once tree-clad. Only in those places throughout Ireland and Great Britian where no trees have ever grown will the once-common Arctic and Alpine flora still survive.

These tough colonists were soon joined by others, but where did the other plants come from? To picture this we have to think about sea levels. When the ice sheets were at their maximum extent and thickness 22,000 years ago, there was so much water locked up in ice all across the Northern Hemisphere and elsewhere that the sea level all over the world was lowered by 120m. This meant that the North Sea and the English Channel were just river valleys and the water levels in the Irish Sea and St George's Channel were so low that in some places tracts of dry land may have been exposed. It may have been these strips of dry land which became the highways along which plants and animals could spread from continental Europe. As the present St George's Channel is deeper than 120m, the exact nature and extent of these land links are still not well understood.

Some plants were able to expand their range from the Mediterranean to southern Britain and into Ireland. Now the 'Great Plant Race' began, for as the weather warmed and plants flourished, the ice melted and the level of the sea was rising fast. What we now know about the changing climate at the end of the glaciation comes from records in the Greenland ice caps, ocean sediments and lake muds and these tell us that the temperature rise was very fast. Some flowering plants made the journey as far as Ireland but others got only as far as Great Britain before the growing sea barrier blocked their journey.

Although the total number of flowering plants growing in Ireland is smaller than that in Great Britain, this does not mean that Ireland's flora is but a reduced sample of species found in greater abundance in Great Britain. There are some fifteen plants growing in Ireland which are found in no other part of the British Isles. Their nearest relatives are found in the Mediterranean region. These unique plants include members of the heather family, especially the strawberry tree (*Arbutus unedo*), an orchid (*Neotinea maculata*, which has also been found in the Isle of Man), two more saxifrages (*S. spathularis* and *S. hirsuta*) and an insect-eating plant (the large-flowered butterwort, *Pinguicula grandiflora*). Collectively these special Irish natives have come to be known as the Lusitanian Flora or Hiberno-Cantabrian flora. The route by which

they arrived in Ireland is not well understood, but it is possible that they spread through areas along the changing coast of the emergent British Isles. The plant 'highway' to Europe has long vanished, swamped by rising seas with the land beyond our present southern shores disappearing beneath the waves almost 9,000 years ago.

The birch is the ideal pioneer tree. The seeds are light, produced in large quantities and transported by wind. A little seedling like this will reach flowering age in only ten years.

The arrival of forest trees

The order in which trees appeared in the new Irish landscape was controlled by how quickly each species could spread and how far from Ireland had been their glacial refuges. The climate had warmed rapidly and stabilised about 11,500 years ago, but it was some time before

For a brief period of a few hundred years hazel became the dominant tree over much of Ireland. Now patches of hazel woodland like this remain only in areas such as the limestone of the Burren.

Tall mixed deciduous woodland took over from the hazel which was then relegated to the status of an undershrub.

the first trees migrated from their southern refuges.

One of the tundra plants that colonised Ireland along with the dwarf willow and the juniper was the dwarf birch. This low twiggy plant is now extinct in Ireland, but the first true trees to arrive in Ireland about 10,500 years ago were also birches, (*Betula pendula* and *B. pubescens*). Their delicate form of growth and distinctive silvery bark distinguish them from all other native trees. Birch, with its light papery seeds and its ability to set seed after only ten years growth, is the ideal pioneer. Today we see it colonizing cut bogs and demolition sites (see Chapter 3). Birch will grow vigorously where there is uninterrupted light so it was well suited to the conditions at the start of this interglacial when it was probably the tallest organism living in Ireland. Birch woodlands contributed much to the developing soils as each year in autumn its leaves made a further contribution to the humus in the soil. Birch does not cast much shade so it was beneath the new canopy of trees that the primroses (*Primula vulgaris*) and anemones (*Anemone memorosa*) may first have blossomed. Birch was accompanied by the damp-loving willows (*Salix* species) as the first of the tall, woody species.

Hazel (*Corylus avellana*), whose arrival was only some 500 years after the birch, shows the importance of light as a controlling factor in plant growth and distribution. Although it is usually only a shrub, seldom reaching more than 3m high, it was able to out-compete the birch and form dense woodlands in the west and north of the country. It was able to do this because the birch seedlings could not grow successfully under the shade of hazel whereas the hazel seedlings could thrive under the birch. However, the days of the hazel 'forest' were numbered because the tall hardwood trees, oak (*Quercus* species) and elm (*Ulmus glabra*), soon arrived in Ireland and hazel reverted to a shrub growing under the forest tree canopy. Oak and elm were well established by 9,000 years ago with Scots pine *(Pinus sylvestris)* already growing on the lower slopes of some uplands.

There is nothing remaining in Ireland that would give an idea of the extent of this primitive forest. Over much of the lowlands, the woodland stretched from shore to shore and even extended up to almost the summit of the highest mountains. The forest was so dense that there were few grasses or flowering plants living under it. The only places where this interminable forest thinned were on areas of limestone rock where the soil was very shallow, on unstable sands and screes, on lake edges and on

There is now nowhere in western Europe where undisturbed oak forest remains. This view of a small island in Lough Erne gives an impression of the view seen by the first farmers to arrive in Ireland almost 6,000 years ago.

the most exposed of mountain tops. The treeless west of Ireland – Donegal, Sligo and Connemara – was all well forested 8,000 years ago and other uplands, now covered by mile upon mile of blanket bog, were also forested.

No remnant of this natural forest persists in western Europe. The nearest parallels are a few areas within managed forests that have been preserved as nature reserves in France. These are within areas of commercial oak forest and completely closed to visitors. There are no paths nor is there any felling or tidying of the forest. They are awesome and frightening places.

By the time the forests had closed over much of Ireland, people had arrived. They were a small population of Mesolithic people relying on hunting and fishing, who lived around the coast and in the river valleys. They had little reason to venture into the dark forests of the interior as their food supply included fish, shell fish and the hazel nuts which were most plentiful on the forest margins. They may also have used a range of other foods such as fungi about whose history, sadly, we know almost nothing.

The two common modern trees, which were still uncommon 8,500 years ago, were the alder *(Alnus glutinosa)* and the ash *(Fraxinus excelsior)*. The alder expanded its population in many parts of Europe just after 8,000 years ago. It had arrived in Ireland somewhat earlier but seems to have been held in check. The changes which occurred to give it a competitive advantage after 8,000 years ago are not clear, but its present habitat in damp places and river banks suggests that a change to a more moist climate may have been responsible for its increase. The ash, on the other hand, waited another 2,000 years before it too became more common and it really gained its present status as the most common native Irish tree only in recent centuries.

Forest destruction

We may criticise poorer countries in the tropics for felling primeval rain forest, while ignoring the fact that in Ireland the same thing started almost 6,000 years ago with the arrival of Neolithic farmers. In those 6,000 years Ireland has gone from 95 per cent forest cover to about 1 per cent forest of native (i.e. not including plantation conifers) trees today. The Neolithic (New Stone Age) people came from central Europe bringing with them a new tool kit. They were farmers used to working in forested regions and had efficient stone axes to fell trees. They knew the value of burning the felled timber to give fertile fields for planting crops. They grew wheat and barley, made decorated pottery, better than any made in Ireland for the next 4,000 years, and built solid houses of oak planks. The area of forest cleared at this time was probably minute, but the process had been started and was either continued by further waves of immigrants or was advanced by new technology introduced from continental Europe.

Later, the new bronze tools, brought in about 2,000 BC, enabled forest clearance to proceed faster and the introduction of iron

Prehistoric stone axe head with a modern handle used in an experiment carried out in Draved forest in Denmark to prove that these tools could have been used by prehistoric farmers to clear forest for crop growing. (Photo: Alan Smith.)

in the last few centuries BC had even more of an impact. Once trees had been cleared from many of Ireland's landscapes, the process was just as irreversible as it is in the rain-forest today. The success of trees in windswept west-coast sites is dependent on mutual shelter, because once some trees are felled, the wind will prevent the establishment of replacements and make the remaining trees more vulnerable.

The uplands, too, changed dramatically as the loss of trees, combined with the high rainfall, led to waterlogging of the soils and the formation of blanket bogs. It now seems highly likely that most of Ireland's blanket bog owes its origin directly to forest clearance by people, mostly in the Bronze Age (about 2,000 to 1,000 BC). It is true that there are plenty of areas of the globe, in Siberia and Canada for example, and in parts of New Zealand which were not settled, where blanket bog formed without help from people, but the tell-tale charcoal from clearance fires that is so common under Irish blanket bog suggests that woodland clearance for farming, combined with trampling and overgrazing, was the direct cause of blanket peat formation here.

One thousand years ago almost all of the dense oak forest had gone; the remaining woodlands were composed of scattered oak with hazel and alder.

The uplands of Ireland, except for the highest mountain tops, were all forested. The blanket peat that now covers these mountains is mostly only some 4,000 years old.

From about AD 800, the monastic settlements in Ireland were influential in agricultural improvements. This early settlement at Nendrum had a tide-powered corn mill.

These cultivation ridges in western County Sligo could pre-date the famine of the 1840s when the population of Ireland was at its maximum. Huge areas of marginal land were then cultivated.

As we move into the later Middle Ages there is some confusion about the amount of woodland remaining in Ireland. Many historical documents suggest that much of Ireland was still wooded, and indeed there was probably extensive untidy scrub of hazel and alder and great tracts of bog. This landscape posed severe problems for the English military attempting to control Ireland, who thus tended to over-stress the amount of impenetrable 'forest' in reports back to England. The botanical evidence suggests that there was little true hard-wood forest left by this time and probably no forest that was not managed and utilised.

The final part of this history brings us up to the present century where the landscape of small fields and hedges is again being modified to meet the needs of mechanical agriculture. The patchwork of small fields is giving way to larger units to suit the needs of larger farm machinery.

How do we know what plants grew in Ireland in the past?

Plants produce pollen, a fine dust that blows in the wind, as hay fever sufferers know only too well. Pollen is the plant's equivalent of sperm, but unlike sperm has no motility and plants depend on wind and animals to transfer the pollen from one plant to another. Most pollen never reaches another plant of the same species and some may land on bogs or settle onto lakes where it sinks to the bottom. Pollen grains are composed of a very resistant substance that survives for thousands of years in wet, oxygen-depleted conditions like peat and lake muds. Each grain is also characteristic of the plant that produces it since pollen is as distinctive to its parent plant as are leaves or flowers. The image below is a scanning electron micrograph of a pollen grain of dandelion which is about 30 thousandths of a millimetre across. We can obtain fossil pollen from peat bogs and from the sediment in lakes and identify which type of plant produced it. Because pollen is produced in such large amounts we can count numbers of pollen grains in each sample and work out the proportions of different plants in the surrounding vegetation. This process is called pollen analysis and has been the key to understanding the story of plant migration, development of forests and the effects of agriculture over the millennia since the last glaciation.

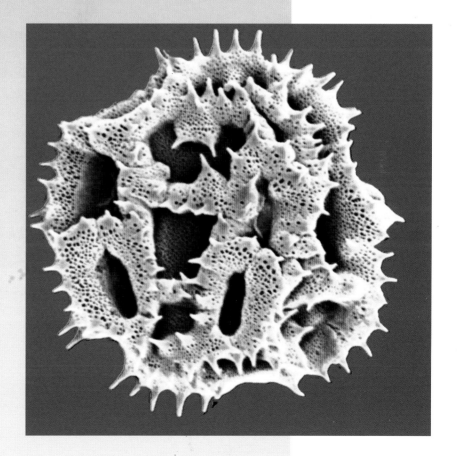

2 WOODLANDS

Types of woodland in Ireland

Ireland has only about 6 per cent of its land area in woodland and all but 1.2 per cent of this is recently planted conifer forest. Although the conifers used for commercial forestry are non-native species, they still provide an important habitat for native fauna. In this chapter we are more concerned with deciduous woodland both in the form of small areas interpreted as remnants of original 'wildwood' and those areas of planted deciduous woodland mostly associated with demesnes. Consideration is also given to the small trees that formed the shrub layer in prehistoric wildwood and now form a component of hedges and scrub woodland.

Parkland oak, Shanes Castle, County Antrim.

Forest oaks, Northern France.

Wood sorrel and violet.

Wood anemone under planted oak and beech.

Bluebells under the dense shade of planted lime trees.

Structure of woodland – layers and light

The key to understanding the plants of woodland and the way they grow is light. Light is the factor that controls tree shape, spacing of trees in woodland and the structure of the shrub and ground flora layers. The effect of competition for light is easily seen by comparing trees grown in dense woodland with the same species in open parkland. It is easy to use non-biological terms such as trees 'reaching up to the light', but the truth is almost as simple. Those branches of a tree that do not receive enough light die. In the open, the horizontal branches will get plenty of light and continue to grow whereas

Primrose on a woodland margin.

Celandine, one of the first spring flowers in Irish woodland.

Cuckoo-pint at a woodland edge.

have not unfurled. This is the opportunity that the woodland spring flowers use: the best known is the bluebell (*Hyacinthoides non-scripta*). The most dramatic bluebell woods are under beech trees in the chalk hills of the Chilterns and Downs in the south of England. The beech casts a much denser summer shade than oak and in mid-summer there is little or no ground vegetation under beech. The bluebell is able to carry out its annual life cycle in the few weeks of spring. One of the reasons for its success as a woodland plant is that it has a bulb containing reserves that allows it to produce both flowers and leaves at the same time. In Ireland, the bluebell usually forms part of a mixed carpet of flowers with the wood anemone, wild garlic (*Allium ursinum*), cuckoo-pint (*Arum maculatum*), celandine (*Ranunculus ficaria*) (all with some form of underground storage) and primroses. All these species were probably less common in the primeval oak forests, where they would have been restricted to the better-lit conditions of the woodland edge. In the more open, managed woodland of the present day, selective felling, coppicing and woodland paths for visitors all let in more light than can have been present under our original primary woodlands. These woodland plants are also seen in the bases of hedges where they survived after all the local woodlands were removed.

the same branches in a woodland tree would die. Thus the shape of the individual trees, and the plants that grow in and below the trees are controlled by the availability of light.

As the natural woodland of Ireland is deciduous, the amount of light on the forest floor varies dramatically through the yearly cycle. There is a brief time in the early spring when temperatures have started to rise although the tree leaves

Later in the summer, when the tree cover is more dense, all that can be seen of the bluebells are the dry seed heads. The celandine disappears completely, resting until the following spring as an underground tuber. The primroses, on the other hand, expand their leaves and continue to grow during the summer, laying down reserves in the roots for the following spring.

Foxglove flowers in mid-summer.

Bilberry flowers in spring.

Bilberry in fruit in September.

Young fern fronds.

Expanded fern fronds.

Hard fern showing vertical fertile and inclined sterile fronds.

Common polypody growing on oak branches.

During the summer it is the ferns and foxgloves (*Digitalis purpurea*) that often dominate the woodland floor in more open areas. Ferns are a primitive, non-flowering plant with two separate stages in their life cycle (see p. 25). The first, the gametophyte, is tiny and fragile, and can survive only in very moist, sheltered soil. From this the second stage, the adult fern or sporophyte arises. It is much more resistant to desiccation and many can even grow quite well in dry conditions. Ferns in woodland show various adaptations to the low light intensity habitat. Most ferns have a structural dilemma. Ferns reproduce not by seeds but by tiny dust-like spores which are produced on the underside of the leaves. For the spores to be dispersed efficiently the leaves should be vertical. The leaves, however, also catch the light and for maximum light absorbing efficiency they should be more nearly horizontal. Some ferns compromise with drooping or curved leaves (for example the male fern, *Dryopteris filix-mas*). Others such as the hard fern (*Blechnum spicant*), for example, have two slightly different designs of leaf: more horizontal leaves with no spores to catch the light and narrower vertical leaves for spore production.

Another solution to the problems posed by lack of light on the woodland floor is to grow higher in the tree canopy. Plants can spend all of their life rooted in the leafy compost which develops on the branches of some trees. Others may have their roots in the ground but send their leaves high in the air as they climb upward to reach the light.

The polypody fern (*Polypodium vulgare*) usually grows in the decomposed leaves trapped in the bark on the branches of trees where the fern causes the tree no harm. Plants that grow in this way are called epiphytes and are different from a parasitic plant such as dodder (see Chapter 6) that

Ferns

Ferns have been on the Earth for many millions of years longer than the flowering plants. The plants commonly called ferns represent one of two stages in the life-cycle of a fern. The leafy fern stage, called the sporophyte, has no sex organs. To produce sex organs, fine dust-like spores are shed from the undersurface of the fern leaf or frond. The spores germinate in damp conditions producing a small pad of delicate tissue on which the male and female sex organs develop. This small, fragile, second stage is called the gametophyte because it produces sexual cells or gametes. After fertilisation, a new sporophyte grows from the body of the gametophyte and the cycle begins again.

5mm

This photo, taken through a microscope, shows a fern gametophyte, the flat fleshy part at the lower right, and the first two leaves of the sporophyte at the top and left.

The tetraploid Irish ivy (variously Hedera hibernica *or* H. helix hibernica) *differs from the common ivy in subtle characteristics, some of which can be seen only with a magnifying lens. Its distribution in Ireland is currently under investigation.*

Ivy showing the juvenile form of the lobed leaves on the climbing stems.

Ivy in fruit in spring with the adult, non-lobed, leaf shape.

grows at the expense of another. Some of the best examples of epiphytic growth of ferns and mosses on tree branches are seen in Irish oak woods where the horizontal branching growth-form of oak, coupled with its corrugated bark, provides ideal rooting places.

Yet another way to reach the light is to climb. Both ivy and honeysuckle (*Lonicera periclymenum*) are woodland climbers that can reach the sunlight and flower at the tops of trees. The lobed leaves so characteristic of ivy are familiar, but the plant is only a juvenile when its leaves are lobe-shaped. Flowering ivy looks very different as,

when mature enough to produce its small lime-yellow flowers and black berries, it has un-toothed, oval-shaped leaves on branches which make a small aerial bush. Ivy is one of very few Irish plants that is truly winter flowering. Many plants will produce the occasional flower out of season, but the ivy has its main flowering season in November and December.

The honeysuckle, one of the few deliciously perfumed native flowers, is a woodland scrambler. Honeysuckle flowers are rarely seen in woodland because these are right up in the crowns of the trees. All that is visible at ground level are the rope-like stems hanging from trees like something from a Tarzan film.

These are some of the strategies that woodland plants use to combat the lack of light: the high-speed plants of spring, those that hitch a lift and those that climb. All are adapted to cope with the lack of light in this special habitat. Most will not survive well outside woodland. Where there has been woodland recently, woodland plants may persist in hedges –

The twisted stems of honeysuckle climbing a willow tree.

One of the redder variants of the dog rose.

Flowering honeysuckle in a hedge.

Fruiting body of the Amanita *fungus on a woodland floor.*

Fruiting bodies of the honey fungus.

may be found on sand dunes, for example, where grazing keeps down competition from more vigorous grasses. It might also be that the more cloudy skies of Ireland allow these plants to expand beyond the habitats normally seen in Great Britain.

Woodland recycling

In addition to light, two more requirements for plant growth are water and mineral nutrients. Plants use simple minerals as nutrients and these are derived from the soil. Each year a large part of the available nutrient supply is locked up in the tree leaves. For the forest to function it is necessary that these nutrients are recycled each year. This is the function of the fungi and bacteria in the soil. They use the organic matter in the leaves to supply energy for their own growth and in the process they liberate the nutrients back into the soil from whence the trees can then re-absorb them. Very little is usually seen of this huge recycling workforce. It is only when the fungi produce fruiting bodies (toadstools or mushrooms) that we get a glimpse of their activity. Each toadstool is only a small part of the enormous network of fungal strands (mycelium) that is active below the forest soil surface. Most of the fungi in the forest live by the breakdown of dead plant material. A few, however, are parasitic and live at the expense of other living plants. One of the most destructive is the honey fungus

honeysuckle, dog rose (*Rosa canina*) and ivy have adapted well to this new environment, but the celandine and wood anemone seldom persist for long once the woodland cover has gone. In certain soils in Ireland, however, the bluebell and primrose grow quite happily in an entirely open habitat. Both

(*Armillaria mellia*), so called because its toadstools smell of honey. The honey fungus kills many species of living trees and then also lives on the dead wood. From a dead stump it sends out thick strands, like boot laces, into the soil in search of new trees whose live wood it exploits to the point of death. It will kill most forest trees and many garden plants also. If a tree dies unexpectedly, peel off the bark and see if the characteristic 'boot laces' are woven beneath.

The major native forest trees

Oak woodland is one of the most beautiful habitats in Ireland. The soft colours of woodland spring flowers and the yellow-green of the expanding tree foliage are unequalled anywhere in the world. This is valued especially because there is so little natural woodland here. Many of the most extensively visited woodlands in Ireland are in fact totally planted. In the north-east, the State forest that has the most visitors is Tollymore, planted in the 1730s on the bare slopes of the Mourne Mountains. The Powerscourt estate on the foothills of the Wicklow Mountains has a similar history. Ireland is the least wooded of the countries of the European Union and although it now has about 6 per cent woodland including planted forests, about 1 per cent of Ireland's land area is deciduous woodland. As we saw in Chapter 1, woodland is the natural vegetation of Ireland along with most of the rest of north-west Europe, and this

The black 'boot-lace' strands of the mycelium of the honey fungus under the bark of a dead oak tree.

woodland is dominated by oak.

The history of oak has been intimately associated with human history throughout western Europe. Oak was the most important building timber right through prehistory, from the arrival of the first farmers (an oak plank house found at Ballynagilly in County Tyrone dates from 3,500 BC) up to the eighteenth century when Scandinavian imported timber became widely available. In many other parts of Europe, some areas of oak forest were protected as royal hunting forests or chases throughout the Middle Ages and these forests have survived more or less intact. The New Forest and Sherwood Forest in England and the great forests of

Correl Glen National Nature Reserve in County Fermanagh contains one of the few remaining areas of native oak woodland in Ireland.

Fontainebleau and Tronçais in France were protected as hunting forests. In Ireland this type of protection was not afforded to woodland, which is not to say that woodland was unimportant. Oak wood provided the house-building timber, the boat-building timber, the timber for fortifications and for trackways, but its use was not controlled in the same way as in other parts of Europe. One measure of the importance of oak in Ireland can be judged from the

One of the huge old oaks in Fontainebleau Forest, south of Paris. This tree is over 400 years old.

Leaves and acorn of the pedunculate oak, one of the two native oak species in Ireland. The long stalk (the peduncle) on the acorn is characteristic of this species.

frequency of Derry (oak) place names in Ireland. Derry is an Anglicization of *doire*, the Irish for oak.

One of the management systems for oak woods in England has been coppicing. Coppice produces a regular supply of small timber by cutting trees close to the ground and allowing them to sprout. The branches are allowed to grow to a useful size for fencing and light building and then cut again – typically every fifteen to twenty years. This was a medieval system of management very much in line with modern conservation ideals. The forest was managed to produce a steady,

renewable supply of useful, small timber and firewood and to provide occasional large timber trees for construction. It was thought until relatively recently that this system was not practiced in Ireland, but evidence has recently come to light that at least a few of the medieval Irish woodlands were managed in this way. Surviving coppice stools have been found in Killarney and in Counties Wicklow, Kildare and Waterford.

Where, in historic times, woodland was used to produce fuel for processes such as iron working, it was essential that an effective renewable management system was used. An iron works would only have had access to a limited area of woodland, but if this was felled and used the enterprise would have been out of business in ten or fifteen years. By operating a fifteen-year coppice rotation it was possible to use only a fifteenth of the forest each year and ensure an unending supply of wood for charcoal production. In England, iron works, rather than being the cause of woodland destruction, actually helped to preserve woodlands. In Ireland, the situation is

the Irish woodlands there seems to have been a subtle genetic change in the oaks. Because of scant management, the best trees have been removed generation after generation, leaving the poorer quality trees to shed acorns and produce the next generation. The genetic stock of Irish oak for timber is thus poor compared with that in the rest of Europe. In France, where oak forestry is almost an art form, the very best trees, the elite trees as they are called, are not

Substantial oak timbers formed the basis of the prehistoric trackway at Corlea, County Longford. Tree-ring dating showed that the track was constructed in 148BC.

more complex as the fate of iron working was much influenced by strife in the mid-seventeenth century.

Oak woodland has survived to the present day in Ireland solely because of either inaccessibility or because of the poor quality of the timber. Largely because of the management history of

felled but are left to set seed for the next generation of forest. Having said that, it must be recognised that our definition of elite trees is from a human perspective – it is those tall straight trees that produce the best timber. It may be that these are not the trees best suited to the Irish environment. For example, they may not

Two elms in the south of England infected by Dutch elm disease in 1973. Both were dead the following year.

be the trees most resistant to our strong winds and may provide far fewer habitats for the epiphytes that form such a characteristic of our woodlands.

Elm is a magnificent forest tree once abundant in Ireland yet next to nothing is known about ancient elm woodlands. Elm was a significant component of the Irish forests along with the oak before the Neolithic farmers arrived almost 6,000 years ago. The elm forests were much reduced exactly at the time that the Neolithic farmers arrived – not just here in Ireland but all over western Europe. Palaeoecologists have argued about this for decades. One line of argument is that the coincidence between the decline in elm and the arrival of the farmers is so strong that the farmers must have deliberately selected the elms for felling, perhaps to provide cattle fodder as young elm

Yellowing leaves of elm in mid-summer. This is usually the first sign of infection by Dutch elm disease.

foliage is palatable to cattle. The other argument is that the scale of elm reduction is so great all over Europe that a small population of farmers could not have achieved such an effect. The last 30 years have seen a further and dramatic reduction in the number of elms in Ireland and Britain due to the Dutch elm disease. Throughout the south of England hardly a single mature elm tree remains. The culprit is a fungal

Under the bark of a dead elm are the characteristic galleries made by the grubs of the beetle that carries the Dutch elm disease fungus.

Leaves and fruit ('keys') of the common ash tree.

disease (*Ophiostoma novo-ulmi*) carried by bark-boring beetles (mainly, but not exclusively, *Scolytus scolytus*). The beetle bores holes in the bark and lays eggs. The grubs which hatch eat the soft nutritious under-bark layer of the tree leaving distinctive tunnels or galleries under the bark. This, in itself, does not cause very severe damage to the tree, but the beetle also carries the lethal fungal disease.

In Ireland, the spread of this disease has not been quite as rapid as in England. It is still possible to see a few large old elms but look for the tell-tale signs of the disease, which in Ireland will often affect only part of the tree.

You will see one branch or one side of the tree with yellow leaves in the middle of summer. This bit will then be completely dead next year and the above-ground parts of the whole tree may be dead a few years later. Trees apparently killed by the disease often sprout from the roots giving a thicket of new stems. These stems are unaffected by the disease for ten to fifteen years. The beetle likes to make the nurseries for its grubs only in trees of reasonably substantial size. Once the stems reach about 5cm in diameter they are again attacked. This means that the elms are permanently kept as a shrub and never reach flowering age so there is no seed production and genetic change. Many palaeoecologists now believe that the reduction in elm population at the time of the Neolithic farmers was also due to a disease like the Dutch elm disease rather than solely to the ravages of the prehistoric farmers. It is strange, however, that the demise of elm is co-incident with the arrival in Ireland of the farmers so it may have been that farming practices contributed to the elm's decline.

The ash tree population expanded late in Irish woodland history and it is not clear that there were ever native Irish ash woods. It is a plant that tolerates the shallow, alkaline soils of the limestone areas and can now form a dense woodland on such soils. The evidence from the pollen record in lakes and bogs suggests that ash was uncommon except in limestone areas such as the Burren. It is possibly the most common hedgerow tree in Ireland today.

Ash tree in winter. The characteristic turned-up ends to the branches make the ash easy to identify when leafless.

The only native conifers in Ireland are juniper (see Chapter 1), yew (*Taxus baccata*) and Scots pine. Until recently we would have claimed that the juniper was only seen in Ireland as a sprawling ground shrub hardly worthy of mention in this woodland chapter. The upright

Upright juniper growing to 3m high on the shores of Lough Derg in County Tipperary. The more usual prostrate form is growing in the foreground.

Mature Scots pine trees with characteristic flat tops, can be distinguished from other conifers by the reddish colour of the upper branches.

junipers growing to 3m on the shores of Lough Derg have certainly changed this view, however, and pose questions about the status of juniper during the woodland phase of the post glacial in Ireland.

Scots pine has a strange post-glacial history. As we saw in Chapter 1 it was an early arrival in Ireland after the end of the last glaciation and it remained as a component of mixed forest along with oak and elm until Bronze Age times. It then seems to have died out from most parts of Ireland and England, but not in Scotland, about 4,000 years ago. A few trees may have hung on in isolated areas until the first millennium AD. For example, there is some evidence of pine on some of the central Irish bogs, e.g., Clonsast near Portarlington, until the first millennium AD and perhaps in Killarney also at about this time. None, however, seems to have survived into the second millennium AD. There are

A layer of stems and roots of Scots pine preserved in Sluggan bog in County Antrim. Tree-ring dating has shown that the pine lived on the bog surface for over 1,000 years.

Section of pine stump showing clear annual rings and a fire scar (arrowed) from an ancient forest fire.

At Sluggan bog, pine wood that grew 6,000 years ago now makes fire-lighting sticks.

Leaves and fruit of hazel.

Young birch colonising cut-over bog behind area used to stack dried turves.

Mature birch on cut-over bog.

many bogs in Ireland where buried pine stumps can be seen (see Chapter 3). These tell of times, principally about 7,000 and 3,900 years ago, when the surface of the bogs was dry enough for colonization by pine. Some of these pine woodlands lasted for 1,000 years or more before being killed by increasing wetness. Pine was the only tree in these bog woodlands which may thus have resembled a modern, single-species conifer plantation. All the Scots pine now in Ireland is from seed or plants from elsewhere – thought to be mostly

Scottish stock. Pine native to the British Isles still persists in the remnants of the great Caledonian forest in Scotland.

Smaller woodland and hedgerow trees

Birch was the first true tree to arrive in Ireland after the end of the last glaciation. It has always been an opportunist and is now the first tree to spread onto abandoned peat cuttings. Through most of Ireland's woodland history, birch has played a fairly minor role and its timber was not greatly valued, being too weak for structural purposes. It is used today in the production of plywood, but not much is grown in Ireland for this purpose. With government directives to forestry to increase the proportion of hardwood planting, significant areas of birch forest may soon appear in Ireland again for the first time in 10,000 years. Unfortunately, this is not likely to be the native birch, but a faster-growing American species.

Hazel, on the other hand, has always had a valued place in the cultural life of Ireland. Hazel woodlands replaced the birch of the early post-glacial forests and remain on some shallow limestone soils up to the present day. The Mesolithic

Multi-stemmed growth-form characteristic of hazel.

Leaves and fruit of alder.

Simple wattle hurdles woven from hazel stems.

Alder on the banks of a river.

stems making it ideal for coppicing. The hazel bushes are cut close to the ground and allowed to sprout. The stems grow until they are 3-6cm in diameter then cut to make long straight poles that can be used as stakes or split and woven into hurdles or other structures. The hurdles also formed the basis of house wall construction as was found at the Early Christian site of Deer Parks Farm in County Antrim. The walls of the house were formed of a double skin of woven hazel rods packed with heather for insulation. Hazel nuts continued to be collected and valued through prehistory, but today it is hard to find a hazel bush bearing more than two or three. Perhaps this is again a case of genetic deterioration – the most prolific bushes would always be those visited for harvesting and any nuts eaten will not form part of the genetic pool of the next generation.

settlers, who lived along the coasts and river valleys, made extensive use of hazel nuts as one source of food along with salmon and shell fish. Throughout prehistory, hazel was used for making hurdles, palisades and trackways. The natural growth of hazel is as a thicket of

Alder can form a substantial tree, and in England was often coppiced along with hazel. In Ireland, alder wood was probably used as firewood and made into charcoal for metal-working furnaces, as in England. Alder is now most commonly seen along river banks and on the edges of lakes but is also a component of damp woodland.

The pollen evidence shows that by 1,000 years ago most of the oak and elm had been replaced by hazel and sometimes alder. Both alder and hazel formed a major part of the scrubby woodlands in Ireland in medieval times.

Mountain ash in the uplands.

Crab apple.

Cherry, Holly and Rowan

The cherry (*Prunus avium*) is not usually thought of as a forest tree, but in some Irish woods it can be a component of oak woodland as can be seen at Kilbroney wood in Rostrevor, County Down. Very little is known of the history of cherry in Ireland. Because the flowers are insect pollinated and produce little pollen there is little evidence for cherry in the post-glacial pollen records. Cherry seeds or stones, however, are claimed to have been found in many archaeological sites, but as the seeds look very like those of the blackthorn or sloe this evidence may not be reliable. The holly (*Ilex aquifolium*) and rowan (*Sorbus aucuparia*) have probably been in Ireland since the early post-glacial, but only became common once the woodland had been thinned for agriculture from about 3,000 BC. The pollen record from the archaeological site

Guelder-rose fruiting in a hedge.

of Ballynagilly in County Tyrone showed that holly and rowan, or perhaps whitebeam (*Sorbus aria*), were two of the trees that recolonised abandoned farmland after the first phase of early Neolithic farming.

A yew tree in fruit.

remains of their fossilized trunks embedded in the peats of the great bogs of central Ireland. Here yews were larger than those commonly seen in Ireland today and additionally these ancient trees lived to a great age. Over 400 rings have been counted on a yew fossilized in Clonsast bog.

Shrubs of woodland margins and hedges

Shrubs are now found mostly in hedges, but were plants of thin woodland and woodland margins. The hawthorn (*Crataegus monogyna*) and blackthorn (*Prunus spinosa*) are the traditional hedging plants in many parts of Ireland (see Chapter 7). The crab apple (*Malus sylvatica*) is relatively uncommon; the true wild apple has a fruit quite a bit larger than the tiny pointed apples of crab cultivars like 'John Downey' that are popular garden ornamentals. The wild apples have now become so genetically mixed with cultivated stock that a true wild crab apple may be impossible to find. The guelder-rose (*Viburnum opulus*) is seen only in limestone areas and stands out in the hedgerows because of its spectacular scarlet berries in autumn. The rose-pink fruited spindle (*Euonymus europaeus*) and the black-fruited elder (*Sambucus niger*) are also shrubs, originally of woodland margins. Spindle is restricted to lime-rich soils, but elder is abundant and thrives in hedgerows and on wasteland.

Yew, the third native conifer, also came to Ireland soon after the end of the last glaciation. Yew has never been a major component of Irish woodland and is relatively uncommon today in the wild. There are, however, a few yew woodlands in Ireland (for example, Reenadinna Wood in Killarney National Park) that have been present for some 3,000 to 5,000 years having replaced an earlier mixed woodland. The size of the ancient yews can be gauged from the

The pretty pink and white flowers of the holly are less well known than the red, winter berries.

Non-native trees

All the introduced trees appear, from the pollen evidence, to have been in Ireland for less than 300 years. Some have naturalised, others, although equally successful once established, have not strayed from cultivation.

Sycamore (*Acer pseudoplatanus*) is a native of Europe, but is not native to either Great Britain or Ireland, yet is prodigiously successful here. After ash, sycamore is now the commonest hedgerow tree in Ireland. It is prolific in its seed production and can form a huge tree. It is considered a weed by foresters because its timber is of little use as a structural timber. In the last century, sycamore wood was used for making many utensils connected with dairying as its fine texture and lack of a strong taste

The spindle retains its bright berries long after the leaves have fallen in autumn.

Spots on sycamore caused by a parasitic fungus (called tar spot). The spots remain on the soil when the leaves rot in the winter and shoot their spores into the air just as the new leaves are opening.

made it suitable for churns, butter bowls, etc. Sycamore may gain greater respect as a timber tree in the future since it is now included in the list of trees for which grants are available for farm forestry schemes. Sycamore timber is now finding a use as veneer for furniture making. Sycamore forms a component of many of the 'natural' woodlands in Ireland having seeded in from nearby estates where it was planted in the seventeenth and eighteenth centuries. It is also spreading into other habitats such as sand dunes and is proving a threat to these habitats.

Beech planted in the eighteenth century in the Powerscourt estate in County Wicklow.

The beech (*Fagus sylvatica*), a common tree of demesnes and city parks in Ireland, is a native European tree that formed extensive tracts of forest on the chalk downs of the south of England where there are still some large areas of beech woodland. Beech was one of the trees that never made the journey to Ireland before the rising sea level cut off the island from the European mainland. It was planted here in many of the Anglo-Irish estates in the eighteenth and nineteenth centuries since it does well in the drier soils of eastern Ireland and regenerates naturally. Whether it would ever have formed substantial areas of forest here had it arrived naturally seems unlikely. It is more likely that it would have formed a small component of a mixed oak forest. In France, beech

Leaves and fruit of beech.

Leaves and fruit of lime.

often forms an understory beneath massive oaks.

The lime (*Tilia cordata*) is another native of the south of England that never made the journey here until brought in the eighteenth century. It is less successful in Ireland than the beech. It will make a splendid tree, but there is little sign that it is able to set seed here and it is seldom seen beyond old estates, parks and city streets.

The conifer forests in Ireland today are the products of state forestry and, to a lesser extent, private commercial forestry. These have come in for criticism as ugly and unnatural, but they are, of course, no more unnatural than fields of barley or the bleak over-grazed moorlands that they often replace. Planted conifer woodlands pass through a phase of very dense growth during which all the ground vegetation is eliminated through lack of light. It is this stage, reached by many conifer forests today, that is so despised by the public. This situation seldom occurs in natural conifer forests where the trees are of mixed age and where more light reaches the forest floor.

In defence of commercial conifer forestry, it has been shown to have a beneficial effect on bird and insect populations and may represent a better use of our uplands than the grazing of

Planted conifers mark the sunrise skyline.

sheep whose main agricultural role may be to attract a government subsidy. Sheep also cause considerable erosional damage to fragile upland soils. The Norway spruce (*Picea abies*), grown as a commercial crop and also our most common Christmas tree, is not a native to the British Isles, but, interestingly, was in Ireland during one of the brief warm intervals during the last glaciation.

Trunks and cones of spruce were found at Aghnadarragh near Crumlin in County Antrim in a pit dug by BP Coal who were exploring the even more ancient brown coal deposits of the area. The spruce was growing there some 90,000 years ago when mammoths roamed the shores of Lough Neagh. There are other finds of spruce cones from ancient deposits in north County Mayo.

3 BOGS AND WETLANDS

Introduction

Throughout this book, environments will be described which have been altered to varying extents by human activity. It is often difficult to discern early activity in, for example, re-grown woodlands or sand dunes and salt marshes. Bogs are different. Extensive areas of lowland raised bogs show plainly the effects of human activity in the form of peat

Section through a bog containing some 8,000 years of environmental history.

harvesting. Vertical cuttings, penetrating to peats which developed many millennia ago, expose large and ancient timbers. These provide evidence for a landscape once dominated by trees. Moreover, the blanket peats of the uplands, which also suffer from the ravages of peat cutting, owe their very existence to human activity some 4,000 to 5,000 years ago.

Ireland has some of the last undisturbed bog in Europe. The local or international visitor, seeing the wet and heathery bog landscape of the west of Ireland in particular, will often remark favourably on this most Irish of landscapes with its summer greens and purples from the flowering heather blending with the reds of the bog mosses and sedges and the brown banks of the peat cuttings. Today, nowhere else in Europe has the extensive bogs which are the most famous feature of the modern Irish landscape. The bogs have a long and varied history and even a brief visit to a cut-over bog in Donegal, where large, pale-grey bog-pine stumps protrude from the bases and sides of the crumbly, brown turf banks, will provide evidence that the

The complex, multi-coloured pool and hummock surface of an undrained raised bog.

treeless landscapes of today have a history rooted in the forests of the past.

The history of modern bog vegetation is revealed by the structure of the bog. It is only the top 50cm of a bog which is alive. The plants sit on the corpses of their ancestors going back as much as 10,000 years. A bog can exist or develop only if its bulk and hence its nutrients are not recycled as in a woodland, but are locked up in the dead plant material. More is known about the history of the Irish boglands than about any other natural habitat because the large body of a bog is more dead than living and within the old waterlogged corpse is the history of the bog, its surroundings and the very climate of Ireland. The seeds, leaf fragments, fossil woods and microscopic pollen grains and spores of ferns, mosses and fungi are preserved, indeed almost pickled, in the acidic, oxygen-depleted waters of the peat. These tiny fossils provide evidence for the changing plant regimes which comprised the bog and the surrounding dry land over which the great mass of the bog crept as it grew upward and outward century by century.

The countries which border the North Sea and Atlantic Ocean also once had extensive boglands but in most places the lowland peats have long ago been cut or drained. Ireland also has lost considerable areas of bogland. Once wood became increasingly scarce, peat was the sole fuel for the family fire and fuel for the many boilings it took to 'finish' the linen on which the economy of the North was almost completely dependent in the eighteenth century. Within the last 200 years, bog covered seventeen per cent of the land area in the Republic of Ireland. This area of bog is now very much reduced by the need for fuel and drainage for agriculture but, if the upland blanket peat is included, relatively undamaged peatland still covers nearly 4 per cent of the surface of the country.

Late summer flowers on a bog surface, the bell heather and the yellow bog asphodel.

The green pools of a treacherous, undrained raised bog are home to the submerged bog moss Sphagnum cuspidatum.

Although 92 per cent of the peatlands have been lost or damaged in Ireland, the situation in the rest of Europe is dramatically worse, so that 51 per cent of all the intact bogland remaining in Europe is in Ireland. Of that area only a fraction, some 23,000ha, is still considered to be sufficiently intact to be worthy of conservation. This precious fragment of a once-huge landscape is the home of beautiful mosses, colourful flowers, insects, birds and mammals like the lithe and elusive Irish hare (*Lepus timidus hibernicus*). Walking over the frozen, heather-clad surface of a bog on a cold winter day and discovering, with some alarm, that the brown, mossy hummock was, in fact, a sitting hare which has risen almost at one's feet and is now leaping as high as a man as it springs across an old abandoned peat cutting, is an exhilarating and unforgettable sight.

The large undrained bogs with their patchwork of pools and hummocks which covered much of the lowlands, even in the early years of the last century, have almost vanished, but there are still a few places left in Ireland today where the classic, wet bog surface remains. Even these best of bogs may be drier than once they were. Bogs now preserved as nature reserves (e.g. Mongan and Clara in County Offaly, Meenadoan and Claraghmore in County Tyrone) have been cut round the edges and the surrounding land has been drained.

There are a number of different types of bog, but in this chapter they are reduced to two main types; the lowland 'raised' bogs and the upland and west coast 'blanket' bogs. These bog types are different, not only in their appearance and in some of the plant associations that grow on them, but also in their origins. This is why this chapter

The bright patchwork of colours on a bog surface comes mostly from the Sphagnum species.

An undrained raised bog is a treacherous place. The open-water pools may be more than 2m deep with nothing solid enough below the water to bear weight, and to add to this danger, there are often floating mats of vegetation over the surface of old pools, just strong enough to bear a person's weight – or perhaps not. There is more water in peat than in milk as peat is at least 95 per cent water; full cream milk is only 85 per cent water.

The three main stages in bog formation are the infilling of open water to form fen, the maturing of the fen into woodland and finally the loss of fen vegetation and the development of a true bog.

From open water to fen

Most of the classic raised bogs started life as a shallow lake or possibly a river flood-plain. Early in this interglacial, some 10,000 years ago, where there are now bogs, there were only shallow lakes. As the climate warmed, the waters of the lakes filled gradually with inwashed soils mixed with the dead bodies of all the tiny, green algae which grew in the shallow, nutrient-rich waters. These new muds were a perfect rooting medium for the larger flowering plants adapted to living in shallow water. These included plants like the white water lily (*Nymphaea alba*), the bur-reeds (*Sparganium* species) and the pond weeds (*Potamogeton* species). Today it is the yellow-flowered water

incorporates lake vegetation for, in the ancient past, the lakes and the great wet flood-plains of the myriad streams and rivers of Ireland were the birthplace of our modern raised bogs.

Raised bogs

The most common bog in the lowlands is the raised bog. It is so called because it has a domed shape, much like an upturned basin, and, when fully developed, rises well above the surrounding landscape.

Plants such as the rushes that are rooted in the mud continue the process of infilling the lake.

Floating plants such as the water lily add dead leaves to the sediment, gradually making the water shallower.

lily (*Nuphar lutea*) which is common in slow-moving water, but it may not have been common in the early lakes. Its fossils are found in the deposits near the bases of a number of bogs in Great Britain but not until the mid-post glacial.

Today the edges of lakes are often fringed by an aquatic rush (*Schoenoplectus lacustris*), but in early post-glacial times the saw sedge (*Cladium mariscus*) was often common on lake margins. The saw sedge needs a lime-rich water and is now quite rare but, in the days before the bogs developed from the young lakes of the limestone rocks of the Central Lowlands, such water would have been plentiful. The saw sedge, so called because of the razor-sharp, serrated edges to the leaves, will not tolerate very cold winters and

Idealised scheme of lowland raised bog formation

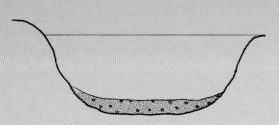

1) *Open water conditions. Little vegetation on the dry land so rain washes sands and clays into the lake.*

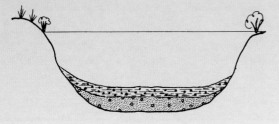

2) *Open water with marginal vegetation starting to grow. Fine organic sediments deposited, mostly remains of algae living in the lake water.*

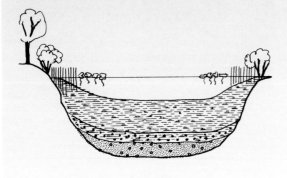

3) *Water depth reduced, reeds advancing towards centre where there is floating vegetation of pond-weeds and water lilies. Willows colonise the margin.*

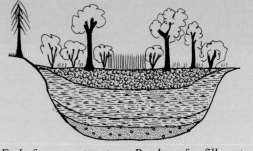

4) *End of open water stage. Reeds or fen fill centre and a wet woodland colonises the margins.*

5) *Wet woodland with some oaks now covers the old lake. Peat accumulation continues above ground-water level.*

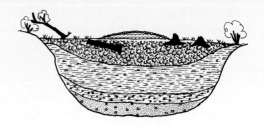

6) Sphagnum *moss increases between the trees and fallen trees are preserved in the peat.*

7) Sphagnum *now covers the whole surface of the bog and starts to form the characteristic domed profile. Margins spread outwards.*

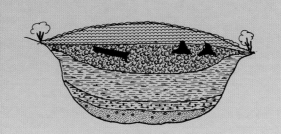

8) *Temporary drying of the surface allows pine to colonise the bog.*

9) *Return of wet conditions kills the pine and the stumps are buried by fresh* Sphagnum *moss.*

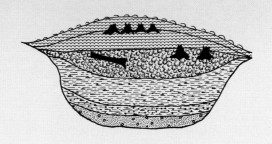

10) *The bog is drained and cut for fuel, exposing the various phases of its history.*

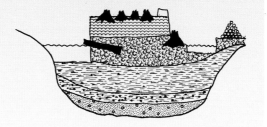

Not all bogs started as open water lakes and not all passed through all the stages shown in these diagrams. Many raised bogs of the Irish Midlands started in river flood-plains rather than lakes while others progressed from reedswamp directly to *Sphagnum* bog. The preserved remains in the peat tell the individual history of that bog.

The full sequence shown here often represents 10,000 years.

The flowering rush on the banks of the River Shannon.

discovery of its fossils in deposits that formed at the end of the last glaciation was one of the pieces of evidence used to infer a rapid rise in temperature at this time. Another lake and river margin plant that may have been much more common in the past is the flowering rush (*Butomus umbellatus*). This also is found only in fairly lime-rich waters. It grows in the quiet, still waters of little inlets such as those which fringe the banks of Lough McNean in County Leitrim and Lough Derg in County Tipperary.

As the ancient lake margin vegetation further reduced the water depth, the lake edges were colonised by reeds (*Phragmites australis*). The reed is the tallest Irish grass, often growing to over 2m high. Each year these tall grasses make huge quantities of stems and leaves which as summer fades, die and collapse into the cold, rising waters of the lake. It is the remains of the reed stems at the bottom of the peat which provide proof that the great raised bogs were once lakes. Today there are still areas on the margins of lakes that are at this stage of development. The reed swamp, which is the parent of the bog, built up such a thick layer of organic debris that soon the lake margin was dry

A small colony of saw sedge in a lime-rich lake in Fermanagh.

Species-rich fen vegetation fills an old lake basin on Rathlin Island.

Marsh cinquefoil (left).

Saw sedge forms tussocks up to 1m high (right).

Debris from lake-margin plants such as these gradually fill the lake with organic sediment.

enough for the wide range of species that form fen. These plants of damp and waterlogged soils may be found in many wet habitats in Ireland – many will be encountered again in the grassland chapter – but are at their most spectacular in fenland. The fenland plants require a reasonably nutrient-rich water supply. Early in the season, the fen colours are blue and yellow with the bright blue of brooklime (*Veronica beccabunga*) and the intense yellow of the marsh marigold (*Caltha palustris*). These flower before the taller plants such as the meadowsweet (*Filipendula ulmaria*), purple loosestrife (*Lythrum salicaria*), the spectacular plum-coloured marsh cinquefoil (*Potentilla palustris*) and the water mint (*Mentha aquatica*) come into flower in mid-summer. The reeds usually remain part

of this fen community which may also contain the saw sedge. Marsh orchids, ragged robin (*Lychnis flos-cuculi*) and lady's smock (*Cardamine pratensis*) give a pinkish flush to the fen in mid-summer. Among this profusion of vegetation there are already clumps of *Sphagnum* moss that will eventually have such an important role in the formation of the raised bog.

In the development of a bog, the open water gave way to fen and as the ground became less wet, water-loving willows formed clumps in the fen, and as this newly-created dry land became stabilised by the willow roots, taller trees such as birch and then oak colonised the fen.

Bogs then were as variable as they are today, so not all raised bogs went through an oak woodland stage but

Lake margin colonised by reeds, Ireland's largest native grass.

many did and the 'bog oaks' are now revealed when the bog is cut or drained. This ancient, wet, oak woodland no longer exists – there are now no bogs in Ireland supporting the sort of woodland that was present in the mid-post glacial, but some insight can be gained into what they must have looked like from the large size of the bog oak timber preserved. Yet more evidence of local variation comes through the other types of fossil timber preserved along with the bog oaks, such as pine and yew. In some of the bogs in central Ireland, great yews also grew with the oaks. These were fine tall trees with strong single-stemmed trunks, unlike the multi-stemmed yew trees common today.

The transition from fen to bog

The next stage of development of the raised bogs distinguished the upper parts of the bog from all other landscape types, for soon the level of the bog

Remains of the underground stems (rhizomes) of reeds in peat showing that this bog was previously a reed swamp.

Bog oaks, bog yews and bog pines

Many types of wood are found in bogs, but there are only three that remain as solid wood. The other woods preserved in bogs like birch and willow become soft and mushy. The three that remain hard are easy to tell apart. When freshly cut the oak is always blackish or grey in colour, the pine is yellowish and the yew is red or pinkish. All go a silvery grey when exposed to the weather. When searching for bog yews among the huge heaps of trees dragged out of Clonsast bog by Bord na Mona, we found that we could tell the difference between the species by hitting the tree trunks with a hammer! The yews rang like a bell whereas the oaks and pines gave a dull thud. All three fossil timbers can be used for furniture, veneer and a variety of craft work. Today this timber is a very under-used resource in Ireland, although some is now being used for ornamental purposes. Most bog timber ends up as firewood or is just burnt in heaps at the side of the bog. In the previous two centuries bog timber was extensively used for cottage roof timbers and other domestic woodwork.

Where the tree stumps are seen in their original situation in the bog they give an insight into phases of drying of the bog and the layers of fresh *Sphagnum* peat that usually buried them tell of a dramatic worsening of the climate that killed the trees. Bog oaks have also provided the all-important ancient tree-ring information that has enabled the building of a tree-ring chronology spanning over 7,000 years.

surface became raised up above the water table; this is the level at which the ground water normally sits – roughly the original lake surface level. Once the bog surface had risen above this level, there were no longer mineral nutrients available from the ground water so the only nutrients to which the bog plants had access were those supplied by rain water.

Rain water is a sufficient diet for some of the mosses, sedges and heathers which were already growing on the surface of the fen. It is at this stage in bog development that the fen woodland started to die as the tree roots became waterlogged. In effect, the tree roots drowned in the water which surrounded them. This was not flood water but water contained within the fabric of the moss plants which engulfed the trees. *Sphagnum* is a

(left) Bog oak trunk tells of prehistoric bog woodland.

Bog pine stumps in pasture that was once bog come to the surface as the underlying peat dries and shrinks (right).

Bog asphodel on a raised bog surface.

Bog cotton give a snow-sprinkled look to a bog in summer.

remarkable moss with an internal structure engineered for life in a very wet environment and with cell walls which are slightly acidic. It is these twin characteristics of water holding and continual acidification of the surrounding water which forced great changes in the bog and its vegetation, especially the death of the fenland trees.

As the *Sphagnum* grew, it pulled its water supply up with it by containing the water inside the wick-like structure of the plant and added to the acidity already developing in the surface water. When the soaking-wet *Sphagnum* grew up and round the bases of the oak trees it killed them by starving the roots of oxygen. The wet, oak woodland was

The patchwork surface of an undrained raised bog showing hummock-forming Sphagnum *species in the centre. The leaves and orange seed-heads are of bog asphodel.*

slowly drowned, to be replaced by the heathers, mosses and sedges which are the plants perfectly suited to life on a true raised bog, always dominated by *Sphagnum* moss.

Changes on the bog

Although wet bogs are treeless today, at times during the last 9,000 years, bog surfaces dried out long enough to allow pine trees to grow on the bog. It is known from tree-ring studies that pine thrived on some bogs for intervals as long as 1,000 years before once again

the wet conditions returned and the surface was dominated by *Sphagnum*. When the bog is cut, the pine stumps and trunks re-emerge. Amongst the ancient pine stumps are well-preserved, fossilized pine cones which are still able to open and shut with changes in moisture, just like modern ones. Not all the bog pines are the same age, but radiocarbon dating of a number of specimens has shown there were extensive pine woodlands on bogs around 7,000 and 3,900 years ago, suggesting that these were drier times in

Ireland's climatic history. Others say that the pine trees which once grew on the bog were all knocked over in the first rush of water in Noah's Flood. A more elaborate version of this story is told in parts of County Antrim, where many bog pines show the scars of ancient fires. It is said by people who know these places well that the Flood waters quenched a raging forest fire before toppling the trees.

Plants of a raised bog

The number of plants that can tolerate the wet and acid conditions of a raised bog is limited, with the greatest diversity of plants among the mosses. On any raised bog there is a range of *Sphagnum* species, all adapted to varying degrees to life in the wet. The bog pools are the domain of limp-stemmed *S. cuspidatum*, sometimes known as 'drowned-kitten moss' for it looks like a pathetic little

Sphagnum moss

Sphagnum *is the key plant in building Irish raised bogs. The closely-packed individual branches and the structure of hollow cells in the leaves gives it the ability to hold a large volume of water. The large photograph shows leaf cells magnified some 400 times. The green cells are photosynthetic but the clear cells are empty and help the plant to hold water.*

Many bogs in Ireland have the local name Red Bog. Red species of Sphagnum *contribute to the red colour of raised bogs.*

The firm, dry, hummocks of the uncommon Sphagnum imbricatum.

bundle of wet fur when removed from its watery home. With this aquatic moss may grow the bog bean (*Menyanthes trifoliata*) with its bluish-green leaves like those of the garden broad bean and its tiny, orange, bean-shaped seeds. The fine strong body of *S. imbricatum* is in complete contrast to the mosses of the bog pools. *Sphagnum imbricatum* is well suited to life in the drier parts of the bog where it can form large hummocks which, in turn, are colonised by many of the other plants of the living bog. *S. imbricatum* is uncommon today but up until perhaps 1,000 years ago it was widespread and often forms the

bulk of peat in Irish lowland raised bogs. The largest native moss in Ireland, the wavy-hair moss (*Polytrichum commune*), is also a bog-dweller and its tall, dark-green stems and feathery-capped, orange spore capsules stand out against the paler colours of the *Sphagnum*.

Growing with the mosses is a range of plants that can also survive in the harsh conditions of the bog. It is noteworthy that the plants of the bog and the plants of the salt marshes have characteristics in common – they are adapted to live in conditions where fresh water may be at a premium! Not so surprising when one considers that on a hot summer's day, the aerial parts of the bog plants are exposed to the drying sun and in the winter the bog surface may be frozen for weeks on end. The thick, waxy leaf-coverings and water-holding structures of many bog plants such as the heathers serve them well throughout the seasons.

The flowering plants which dominate the raised bogs are the heathers and the sedges. There are three heathers common on Irish raised bogs, with ling (*Calluna vulgaris*) universally present. This low, many-stemmed, evergreen shrub can grow vigorously despite the drying stresses of sun or

This bog pine, exposed by peat cutting, grew when the bog surface was relatively dry.

frost. *Calluna* does well on the drier parts of the bog and grows best on the moss hummocks. When all the ling is in flower in late summer it is a spectacular sight as the bog blushes pink and purple in the summer sun. The exuberant summer flowering of the ling may be more striking now than ever before as drainage and cutting over the last few

Cranberry typically grows on a lawn of Sphagnum.

Bog bean indicates a very wet bog surface.

Plants of drier bogs and bog hummocks:

Heather or ling.

Lichen Cladonia coccifera.

Moss Racomitrium lanuginosum.

Bell-heather.

centuries have provided it with ideal growing conditions. Close relatives of the ling, the bell heather (*Erica cinerea*) and the cross-leaved heath (*E. tetralix*) are smaller shrubs and have distinctive pink to purple balloon or bell-shaped flowers. Either species can normally be found growing in close proximity to their larger relative.

The sedges which dominate the lowland raised bog belong to the Cyperaceae family, and contain many species which may be challenging to differentiate. The bog cottons

(*Eriophorum* species), however, are easy to recognise. Two species, *E. vaginatum* and *E. angustifolium* are common on bogs throughout the country. They do well even in extremely wet conditions and, when in flower, they smother the bog in a carpet

Blanket peat covers old walls and prehistoric settlements on land that was once farmed.

Upland blanket peat can form on quite steep slopes as here in the Mourne Mountains.

On the west coast of Ireland, blanket bog extends right to the sea – to the cliff edge as here or joining the seaweed-covered strand line in sheltered bays.

of downy-white blossoms, as though snow had returned to the bog in late spring. The white flowers of the bog-cotton contrast with the dark leaf sheaths of another common bog sedge, *Schoenus nigricans*. This tough and resilient plant can survive weeks of submergence but, in common with many plants of the bog, will not tolerate shade. It is well-suited to life on the wet, western peats and its tough stems were once used for thatching in south Connemara.

As well as the heathers, grasses and sedges, other plants like the bog rosemary (*Andromeda polifolia*), and the cranberry (*Vaccinium oxycoccos*) straggle over the *Sphagnum* hummocks. Both are uncommon natives and susceptible to changes in the bog's water balance. The bog asphodel (*Narthecium ossifragum*) is one of the few yellow-

The round-leaved sundew with sticky glands on the leaf margins.

Close-up view of the long-leaved sundew.

The long-leaved sundew forming a floating carpet on a raised bog pool.

flowered plants commonly seen growing in bogs where it may form dense patches. It is a most attractive, lily-like plant whose flowers have a faint smell similar to a carnation. It has a bad reputation amongst farmers who grazed livestock on bogs as it was said to make animal bones brittle – hence its Latin name of *ossifragum* or 'broken bone'. Until recently thought to be little better than an old wives' tale, new research has supported the observation that eating the stems of the plant will indeed adversely affect bone strength as the plant contains a chemical injurious to bone.

Many plants are well suited to life in the bog but some have particular strategies which enable them to supplement their scant nutrient supply. Of the nutrients which are in short supply in bogs, nitrogen is probably the most important. It is ironic that nitrogen gas is the most abundant element in our atmosphere, yet in this form it is not available to most plants. One group of plants that has evolved a strategy to overcome a shortage of nitrogen is the

The yellow flowered hemi-parasite cow-wheat on the surface of a drained bog. This is also a plant of woodlands.

insectivorous plants. They capture insects, dissolve them and use the nitrogen compounds from the insect bodies for their growth. One such plant is the sundew, of which there are three species in Irish bogs; round-leaved – *Drosera rotundifolia*, long-leaved – *D. intermedia* and great sundew – *D. anglica*. On its leaves, the sundew has long hair-like glands, each with a blob of sticky mucilage, which trap insects. Once prey has been caught, the hairs curl inwards, drawing the insect into the centre of the leaf where it is dissolved and utilised by the plant. The leaves trap a range of small insects and it has been observed that the numbers

The insectivorous butterwort catches insects on its sticky leaves.

The uneven surface of mountain blanket peat being investigated by plant ecology students. Under 1.5m of peat they found charcoal and the roots of pine trees from an ancient woodland.

micro-organisms with similarities to both fungi and bacteria) to capture atmospheric nitrogen. The bog myrtle (*Myrica gale*) is an example of a bogland plant which houses the nitrogen-fixing actinomycete in nodules on its roots. Nitrogen gas in the air penetrates the top few centimetres of the bog and is metabolised to a form that the bog myrtle can utilise. The well-nourished bog myrtle often stands out as the greenest plant on the bog in late summer when the bog surface nutrients are at their lowest. During autumn many bog plants draw nutrients from the leaves for storage in the roots and underground stems during the winter and eventual recycling the following spring. Another strategy for coping with a poor supply of nutrients is to steal some from another plant. Parasitic plants steal all their requirements from another, but there is a group called hemi-parasites that can survive on their own, but usually cannot set seed without stealing from a host. They form a connection by their roots onto the roots of a host plant and extract nutrients in this way. Two examples found on Irish bogs are the cow-wheat (*Melampyrum pratense*) and the lousewort (*Pedicularis sylvatica*). Both are said to have various hosts but are most often found in association with heathers.

of thrips, ants and beetles caught in a season must be prodigious. In addition to the sundews, there are also the butterworts (*Pinguicula species*). Their sticky, buttery-yellow leaves also trap small insects and, like the sundews, the leaves of the butterworts have glands scattered over their surfaces which exude digestive juices capable of reducing an insect to a nutritious fluid in days.

Other plants harness the power of bacteria and actinomycetes (a group of

Blanket bogs

The other main type of peatland is found on poorly-drained land where the rainfall

Bog myrtle shows up against the browns and purples of a bog in summer.

Lousewort, a hemi-parasite common on drier blanket bogs.

The bog railway and drainage ditches in this County Tipperary bog show the scale of present day peat excavation for electricity generation.

is high. It is known as blanket bog as it hugs the contours of the land like a blanket. While not a hard and fast rule, blanket bog is usually found where the annual rainfall is greater than 1,000mm.

Possibly all the areas that are now covered by blanket bog in Ireland once grew forest or woodland. What happened to turn the great upland forests of the prehistoric period into bleak and treeless bog? The answer is by no means clear-cut. There have been many pollen analytical investigations of blanket bog in Ireland aimed at tracing the changes in vegetation at the transition from woodland to bog. Commonly the pollen record shows there was a period of farming separating the woodland phase from the start of the bog and, most significantly, there are frequently traces of charcoal just beneath the start of the blanket peat, showing that the woodland was burnt. The picture is one of woodland clearance by prehistoric people, burning of the cleared trees and scrub and then the development of pasture with cereal crops grown on some of the better ground. The loss of the trees had, however, a detrimental effect on the forest soils which were compacted by grazing animals and eventually waterlogged leading to the abandonment of the farmland.

The compacted soil and the high rainfall provided the ideal habitat for *Sphagnum* to grow and smother the abandoned fields. The blanket peats of the uplands and wet western lowlands may hide many secrets. Under the blanket peat in the Ceide fields area of North Mayo, archaeologists have been able to uncover 5,000 year-old field walls. The part played by climate change in the initiation and acceleration of the development of blanket bog, some time in the fourth millennium BC, is still not clear even after some 50 years of research. Dramatic climate change alone cannot be

Peat harvesting by tractor-drawn machinery leaves little surface vegetation.

responsible for the start of blanket bog as it then would have started at about the same time everywhere, and this is certainly not true. Most of the radiocarbon dates for the initiation of blanket bog from sites across the country fall between 5,000 years ago and 2,000 years ago, but there is plenty of variation even within a single region such as the Wicklow Mountains or the Antrim Plateau.

Many of the same plants that live in the raised bogs are also present in the blanket bogs, but the grasses, sedges and rushes are more abundant. The heath rush (*Juncus squarrosus*) is a tough, wiry plant of upland blanket bogs. It is an aggressively competitive plant that grows up between other plants then presses its

Drained bog often leaves little trace of its origins.

Cleared and fertilised fields stand out in a blanket bog landscape.

leaves out in a rosette, flattening its neighbours. Often with the heath rush is the equally tough mat-grass (*Nardus stricta*) and the larger, wiry, blue-tinged purple moor-grass (*Molinia caerulea*). As with the raised bogs, however, the main bog-building plant in blanket bog is the *Sphagnum* moss.

Bog destruction

Much was made in the opening paragraphs of this chapter about the shrinking acreage of uncut bog in Ireland. Numerous activities have reduced the amount of bog over the recent centuries and especially during the closing years of the second millennium AD. In the past, bogs in Ireland have either been considered as a hindrance to farming, to transport or to military activity or have been viewed more favourably as an exploitable fuel source. It is not known when peat was first used as a fuel in Ireland, but presumably it was not widely used while wood was still freely available. In the last few hundred years, peat cutting has become an integral part of the rural life and culture of Ireland, appearing in art, poetry and song. Cut and dried peat, known as 'turf' in Ireland, was essential for many operations in the production of linen, starting in the early eighteenth century. Turf cutting was essentially a family activity involving the women and particularly the children in a way that neither modern peat harvesting nor any modern agricultural activity does.

The conservation of bogland, even that damaged by cutting, has been a contentious issue in Ireland in recent decades. From a conservation viewpoint, any peat cutting could be considered as environmental damage, but traditional peat cutting from a vertical peat bank progressed relatively slowly and usually allowed the bog flora to regenerate on the cut areas. More damaging were the

Although Sphagnum *builds up bogs many metres thick, it grows quite slowly and recovers slowly from disturbance and damage.*

Forest plantation on cut-over bog has variable success with many trees suffering from lack of nutrients and others subject to wind-throw because of shallow rooting.

long drains often put into the surface in the middle of raised bogs to try to reduce the surface wetness prior to peat cutting. This manual peat cutting, even on the scale required to fuel the linen industry, was on a minute scale compared with the exploitation of large areas of bogland for electricity generation from the 1950s. This is essentially an open-cast mining operation. The bog is first drained by regularly spaced ditches 2m or more deep. These are left to bleed water out of the bog for several years before peat removal starts. A whole range of machinery was developed in Ireland to harvest the prodigious amounts of peat needed for power-station fuel. Remembering that the freshly-excavated peat is over 90 per cent water and the carbon content of dry peat is still only fifteen to twenty per cent, the volumes of peat required compared with a coal-fired power station are huge. In addition to electricity generation, Bord na Mona also produce peat briquettes – a highly compressed peat for domestic fuel.

As well as the loss of bogs to the power industry, inroads into the remaining bogs have been made for the supply of horticultural peat. This is used as their main growing medium by almost

It is usually the sedges that first colonise a damaged bog surface.

Here fast-growing sedges carpet a recently drained and damaged bog.

all the big horticultural plant producers in Europe. The peat is milled to a consistent size and, with the addition of accurately controlled nutrients, provides the totally reliable and consistent medium required for factory-style horticultural production. The Netherlands, one of Europe's largest plant producers, now relies on importing peat from Ireland, Poland and further afield. The horticultural peat industry prefers the upper, more *Sphagnum*-rich peats. These are milled in the summer and the crumbled peat left to dry on the bog surface from where it is sucked up by giant vacuum cleaners, taken to a factory and compressed into sacks.

The third way in which bogs are now disappearing is the smaller-scale mechanised cutting for domestic fuel. No longer is the family cutting its winter fuel supply by hand, but in a few days one man with a tractor may extract enough peat for his family and excess to

The use of bogs as a dumping ground is still common.

sitchensis) and lodgepole pine (*Pinus contorta*) would tolerate these acid, nutrient-poor peat soils after they had been drained. Further loss of bogland results from draining for farming. Garry Bog, once the largest bog in the north of Ireland, is now productive grazing for cattle. Only about twenty per cent of the original area of bog remains, with a few hectares still retaining its original pool and hummock surface. In many parts of Ireland where drainage and peat cutting have exterminated the bogs, the fact that there were once bogs must be deduced from clues in the landscape. For example, roads raised up above the surrounding landscape often run on top of the last dry remnants of cut bogs. Sometimes the presence of bog oaks and other ancient wood protruding from the field surfaces are all that remains to show where bogs once covered the landscape. A fine example of the speed with which part of a bog can become a field was observed near Sluggan bog in County Antrim. In 1996 we saw a small area of birch and heather-clad cut-over raised bog cleared, the surface fertilised and sown with grass seed. In 1998 it was grazing for cattle.

sell. As the tractor compresses the surface and drags up the underlying peat, the surface vegetation is destroyed. Tractor cutting can ruin many hectares of bog vegetation in a few days. This is a particular threat to blanket bogs as these tend to be somewhat drier than the raised bogs and provide easier access for tractor machinery.

Forestry and farming on peat

Shallow blanket peat-covered uplands have been extensively drained for forestry plantation, once it was discovered that Sitka spruce (*Picea*

'Used bogs'

Large areas of land once covered by raised bog remain unused in central Ireland after mining for power generation. There have been plans and good intentions including ambitious but as yet unrealised schemes to turn these areas into the vegetable and salad production centre for a huge European market. Forestry has also been attempted, but many of the worked-out bogs still seem to grow little but old refrigerators, cars and even the occasional serviceable wheel-chair! Areas remaining after cutting in the traditional way are very different. Here re-colonisation follows the cutting as only small areas are stripped bare each year. The opening of deep cuttings produces pools and areas of fen. Cutting by hand actually increases both plant and animal diversity. It also displays the bog in section both for the palaeoecologist to study and as a salutary display of the ephemeral nature of our own existence. You can stand in front of a vertical peat section that covers the whole of human history in Ireland.

There are few more sad sights than to see an Irish bog, stripped of all its vegetation, being milled and put into sacks to be used to make soil for golf courses in middle-eastern deserts.

4 GRASSLANDS

Throughout most of this interglacial, grasslands have not formed part of the natural vegetation of Ireland, or of most of north-west Europe for that matter. Today, Ireland is famous for a green landscape dominated by grasslands which are almost exclusively the product of agriculture. Farming began during the Neolithic period, and the grasslands expanded in the Bronze Age in response to a growing population and their need for food. The present extent and character of grasslands was greatly influenced by the new agricultural practices of the eighteenth century. The history of the Irish grasslands is well illustrated through pollen analysis and throughout the country the pattern of grassland expansion over the last 5,000 years has been traced.

Pollen analysis and the documentary record show that the present extent of grasslands in the lowlands is a relatively modern aspect of our landscape. During the late seventeenth and early eighteenth centuries, the scrub woodland which was part of the previous grassland system was probably thinned and more extensively grazed, thus reducing regeneration and eventually producing

Stone walls provide shelter for small pasture fields in upland farms.

Grassland on roadside bank with fragrant orchid and twayblade.

the smooth, almost treeless, green landscape which is characteristic of large areas of the lowlands today. In contrast, the upland slopes were always more open and had been changed to grazing land long ago, as a consequence of the ancient practice of taking cattle into the hills for summer pasture.

The types of grassland which developed as pastoralism increased were a product of soil type, climate and the human hand. There are few clear distinctions between each type of grassland, even where soil types vary, as many native Irish plants can live in a range of environments, but one, the species-rich limestone grassland, does indeed stand out visually even at a distance on account of its distinctive and well-nourished green.

Irish grasslands at the end of the last glaciation

The last time there were extensive natural grasslands in Ireland was during the final stages of the last glaciation. There are no modern equivalents to these late-glacial grasslands remaining in Ireland, but they probably looked much like the grasslands of parts of Canada or Russia today. There was a time near the end of the last glaciation when the temperature had risen almost to present-day levels, yet there were few

Without the grazing of cattle most of Ireland's grassland would revert to scrub woodland in only a few years.

Antler and part of the skull of a giant Irish deer. They became extinct in the sudden cold spell about 11,800 years ago having roamed the Irish grasslands near the end of the last glaciation.

trees because there had not been enough time for them to migrate back from their refuges in southern Europe. In Ireland at this time, most of the lowlands were covered by species-rich grasslands where grasses, rushes, sedges and flowering herbs grew in profusion for more than 1,000 years. These flower-speckled meadows provided plentiful food for the giant Irish deer which flourished in great numbers, especially in the plains of Limerick, but then the climate flipped back to glacial conditions and remained so for a further 1,000 years. With the return of the intense cold, the extent of the grasslands was greatly reduced and the giant Irish deer became extinct in Ireland and throughout much of Europe.

The reason for the sudden climate collapse is now thought to have been due to catastrophic disruption of the ocean currents that drive the Gulf Stream. The mechanisms that drive the ocean currents are complex and rely on differences in both temperature and salinity between the polar and tropical waters. New findings show that, as the climate began to warm, huge quantities of fresh water were produced from the melting of the great ice sheet over North America. When this fresh water flooded into the Atlantic Ocean, the delicate balance of salinity that helps to drive the ocean currents was destroyed. That such a ruinous change in climate can be caused by changes in ocean currents should be a warning to us that equally dramatic changes may follow the global warming that we are causing now.

Modern grasslands

Some types of grassland which are present in Ireland today will be described: wet and dry meadow, and roadside and upland grasslands. These

Sheep-grazed rough upland grassland on limestone soil with improved pasture in the lowlands.

each type of grassland may almost imperceptibly blend into any other. About 65 per cent of the land area of Ireland is grassland and if fields of cereals, which are, of course, only annual crop grasses, and amenity grass such of golf courses and lawns are included then this figure rises to about 85 per cent. Ninety-three per cent of agricultural land in the Republic is grassland and 92 per cent in Northern Ireland. This grassland is the basis of the agricultural wealth of Ireland, but in this chapter the main concern will not be with improved agricultural pasture or cereal crops, just with those grasslands that are rich in grass species and the many flowering herbaceous plants which grow in intimate mix with the grasses.

are artificial categories, created by humans to facilitate study or description, for no such clear distinctions are as readily discernible in the landscape, as

A walk through a field of grasses and meadow flowers in early June under

COMMON GRASSES OF IRISH LOWLAND GRASSLANDS

Cock's-foot   *Rye-Grass*   *Sweet vernal-grass*   *Cat's tail*   *Meadow foxtail*   *Crested dog's tail*   *False oat-grass*   *Yorkshire fog*

Grass structure

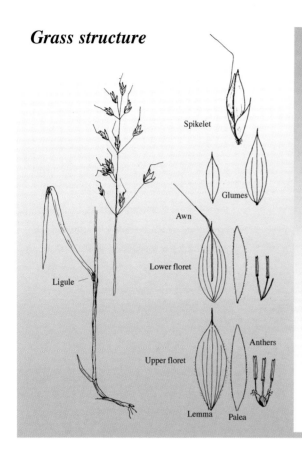

Spikelet

Glumes

Awn

Lower floret

Ligule

Upper floret

Anthers

Lemma   Palea

Grasses are flowering plants that belong to the group of families called the monocotyledons that includes the sedges, lilies and irises, orchids and others. The grasses may be distinguished from the rather similar sedges because grass leaves are arranged in two rows opposite each other on a usually rounded stem. Sedge leaves are arranged in three rows on the stem and the stem thus tends to be triangular in section. Grass flowers are pollinated by wind and have no need for showy petals to attract insects. The various pink and purple colours of grass flowers are mostly the colours of the pollen-bearing anthers.

Identification of grasses requires a knowledge of the specialised terminology – glumes, paleas, awns, ligules etc., as shown in the illustration of the false oat-grass opposite, but most of the common Irish grasses are easy to recognise and identify with the assistance of an illustrated flora.

a sunny sky with the larks singing and the grasshoppers jumping from stem to stem is an unforgettable experience. Initially all the grasses seem to look alike, each made up of long leaf-clothed stems and with a floppy top which may be tinged pink, purple, light-green or beige. On closer inspection the individual grass species are just as distinctive and beautiful as the more brightly-coloured flowering herbs which are the grasses' companions. Grasses are fully-fledged flowering plants, having many of the parts which make up the flowers of the more showy species in the

Seeding grasses in a damp lowland pasture catch the morning sun.

meadow. The individual flowers of most native Irish grasses are small and insignificant until gathered into a flowering head or infloresence. These have distinctive shapes of which the grasses' common names may be accurately descriptive. For example, the flower of the dog's tail (*Cynosurus cristatus*) is one-sided, stiff and bristly along its length. In the early dawn light, the hazy, pink flowers of a field dominated by Yorkshire fog (*Holcus lanatus*) uncannily mimic a rising mist.

Some native grasses in flower are so pretty that they are prized by gardeners and flower arrangers and none more so than the quaking grass (*Briza* species) whose crinkled flower stems are forever moving and shimmering in the slightest breeze. To see quaking grass in profusion a visit to the Burren in summer is advised as quaking grass grows best on limey soils. The common and much more widespread cat's-tail

(*Phleum pratense*) and meadow foxtail (*Alopecurus pratensis*) have unmistakable solid, cylindrical infloresences. Every bit as distinctive is the chunky flower-head of the cock's-foot (*Dactylis glomerata*). Learning a little of the structure of grasses and the names of the most common and easily recognisable will add greatly to the pleasure of a walk in any part of Ireland.

Ireland's grasslands are probably unique as they are the product of a complex interaction between ancient and recent human activity and our exceptionally wet climate. Though much of the rocks of central and western Ireland are rich in limestone and therefore one might expect that they would support grasslands in which lime-loving species would predominate, no Irish grassland resembles the dry, chalk downlands of southern Britain. In Ireland, millennia of exposure to almost daily rain leached much of the soluble

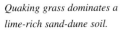
Quaking grass dominates a lime-rich sand-dune soil.

Yellow rattle

Eyebright

Yellow rattle and eyebright are hemi-parasitic on the roots of grasses. They belong to the same family as the cow-wheat and lousewort described in Chapter 3.

Yellow rattle

calcareous material from the surface rocks and allowed the development of soils which were unexpectedly acidic in character. In these places, plants which need a limey soil may grow very close to those which demand acidic conditions. These soils support a wide range of grass species which stock like to eat including some like rye-grass (*Lolium perenne*), cocksfoot, cat's-tail and dog's tail as well as Yorkshire fog, which cattle find unpalatable as it has broad hairy leaves.

The other great influence on Ireland's grasslands is the continuing practice of allowing cattle to graze all year round. The mild, moist climate of most of Ireland lets grass grow even during the depths of winter – gardeners in Ireland will often give their lawns a final cut some time around Christmas. As grass is relatively plentiful and lengthy periods of frost in the lowlands rather rare, it has been the practice of Irish farmers over the centuries to keep cattle outside all year round. In many less-favoured parts of Britain, hay had to be made during the summer and fed to cattle when fresh grass was not to be obtained. Hay making may be a

Field scabious in the Navan Fort grassland.

Dry grasslands on banks of the archaeological site of Navan Fort in County Armagh.

relatively recent addition to Irish agriculture, possibly introduced by Norman settlers 1,000 years ago. One may ask, why make hay when the fresh and more palatable alternative is readily available and why try to dry fresh grass in a climate where trying to dry anything is a risky business.

It is probable that extensive tracts of grassland in Ireland may never have been ploughed and that the plants that grow there today are the descendants of those which first colonised the newly-cleared forest soils over 5,000 years ago. Possibly the best example of the great undisturbed grasslands are those of the Curragh of Kildare which are as rich in fungi as they are in species of flowering plants. The Curragh's fungi are to be found only in pasture which has been undisturbed for many centuries or longer. These ancient and undisturbed grazing lands contrast with the English

hay meadows which may have been ploughed as part of a different agricultural system in which arabalism and pastoralism were sequential rather than separate, which seems to be the Irish way.

When hay was first made in Ireland and when and where the practice became widespread is a contentious issue with agricultural historians. There is very little reference in the early Irish written records to hay making and, where hay was made, it may have been for animal bedding rather than fodder. In addition, there were no ancient farm tools specific to making hay. The careful management of grasslands which are always wet during the winter and may also be so during a typical Irish summer has produced a grassy landscape which is dependent on control of stocking levels and grazing pressure. This management system may have reached almost a high art-form during the early Medieval period when the cattle herds were so large that the hides from surplus stock were used to make vellum for the Scriptoria of the Irish monasteries. Very little is known about the production of vellum in those days, but the few monastic texts which remain from the seventh century and later are evidence of the excellent hides which were to be obtained from the cattle which grazed the splendid Irish grasslands of those days of saints and scholars and the farmers on whom they depended.

Most of the pea family including clover (here) contribute to soil fertility by fixing atmospheric nitrogen. The micro-organisms that carry out this valuable task live in the small whitish nodules on the roots.

Wet grasslands

What therefore makes Irish grasslands so lush and unique? The wet grasslands take many forms and may be found throughout the country but one type stands out as different from all others. Throughout the British Isles there are water meadows, which in Ireland are known as callows (*caladh*). The best–known Irish examples of these species-rich grasslands are the low-lying fields along the River Shannon, but they are also found along many similar rivers. Where fields are frequently flooded in winter, often with a considerable depth of water, the water drops silt, bringing an annual renewal of fertility as in the famous fertile areas along the River Nile. Each year these pastures are left to grow a crop of grass which is cut for hay in the late summer – usually at the end of August or the beginning of September.

After this they are grazed for as long as the land is dry enough to keep the cattle on it.

In addition to the grasses, many of the plants that grow on the callows survive because they can complete their

The flood-plain of the River Shannon, close to the site of the monastic settlement of Clonmacnoise, has some of the most famous wet grasslands in Ireland.

In mid-summer the sweet-scented meadowsweet dominates much of the callows grassland.

The butterfly orchid stands out against the dark foliage and seed-heads of the black bog-rush.

life cycle and shed seed before the hay is cut. The autumn grazing keeps the grasses short so that they do not detrimentally shade the flowering herbs the following spring. Of course, none of this is done to promote the flowers; it is one aspect of the complex system of farming developed over the centuries to make best use of a very damp pasture. The riverside meadows are too wet to plough and too wet to grow a useful crop even if they should be ploughed.

The herbs of the grassland make a great contribution to its overall grazing quality and none more so than the clovers (*Trifolium* species) which are prized as they are nutritious and can withstand trampling. No other grassland herb is so valuable or nutritious an addition to the grazing potential of these grasslands. The many types of buttercups (*Ranunculus* species) which are abundant in wet as well as dry pasture make no contribution to the grazing value because they are mildly poisonous.

What then are the plants which so characterise the callows? There are no unique callow grass species nor exotic species of flowering herbs but rather a mixture of plants whose life cycles are in tune with the farming regime. The plants of the callows include many such beauties as the native orchids, lady's smock and meadowsweet and others like the rushes and the sedges which are less showy but just as fascinating when examined in detail.

If the regime of hay cutting in the callows is replaced with silage cutting earlier in the summer then many species soon die as there is not time for the annual herbs to set seed. If the fields are abandoned and neither cut nor grazed the grasslands will soon disappear as they are colonised by alder and willow and eventually turn into a fen or wet woodland. The callows grasslands thus depend completely for their existence on a particular agricultural management system which makes them as much a tangible part of Ireland's heritage as the prehistoric tombs or medieval tower houses, for they are truly a part of the historic cultural landscape.

Wet grazing is not restricted to the callows as Ireland's moist climate supports other types of grassland not dependent on annual inundation by river water. Patches or more extensive areas of wet grassland are common where drainage is sluggish.

Some of the plants which grow abundantly by the banks of streams and lakes grow also in the wetter meadows. In parts of the west, especially in Fermanagh and Leitrim, the fields in May are turned to gold as the marsh marigold bursts into flower. The large glossy golden flowers and thick shiny leaves of this our largest native 'buttercup' grow so densely that each plant almost touches its neighbour. Today in some country areas in Ireland, stems of the marsh marigold – the Virgin Mary's Gold – are still placed across the threshold on May Day. As the year progresses the later-flowering buttercups, like the meadow buttercup (*Ranunculus acris*), or creeping buttercup (*Ranunculus repens*) take the place of the marsh marigold. The longer

Lady's smock in a damp lowland pasture.

Buttercups almost oust the grasses in this frequently-flooded lakeside pasture.

flowering season of the later buttercups will ensure a golden haze throughout the summer and into the cooler days of autumn.

A little later in May, as the marsh marigold completes its flowering for another year, the landscape becomes spattered with pink, first with the lilac-pink flowers of the lady's smock and later with the dusky hues of the ragged robin. The pretty lady's smock belongs to the same plant family as the cabbage and the Brussels sprout and this relationship is not in doubt if the flowers of either vegetable and those of the lady's smock are compared. Each flower has four petals forming a cross – the origin of the family name, Cruciferae.

The dry grasslands

The dry grasslands are in contrast to those which fringe the banks of the lakes and streams of the Irish midlands and may range from farm pasture, that is not re-seeded or heavily fertilised, to some unique conservation area grasslands. Included in dry grasslands are golf courses, roadside verges and even football pitches. An extreme dry grassland habitat in sand-dunes is described in Chapter 6. Many of these grasslands, in common with the water meadows, are artificial and are maintained by a particular farming or maintenance regime. Because the dry grasslands do not present the farmer with problems of waterlogging they are much more amenable to agricultural improvement: therefore the most species-rich dry grasslands that remain are all in places where access for machinery is difficult.

Some of the best examples are on the steep esker ridges, especially in the midlands. These winding ridges of river gravels, formed under the ice of the last ice age, are too steep to plough and have survived much as they may always have been. The Esker Riada is close to the monastic site of Clonmacnoise and also close to the callows of the River Shannon, making this area one of the richest and most varied grasslands in the country. In spring, amongst the first grasses to flower is the fragrant sweet vernal-grass (*Anthoxanthum odoratum*)

Ragged-robin paints these rushy wet pastures vivid pink.

Marsh marigold, usually an occasional riverside plant, sometimes spreads into damp pasture.

with its unmistakable smell of new-mown hay. The other perennial grasses soon follow, along with the mixture of herb species which is part of the glory of the Irish spring countryside.

One of the loveliest and most easily recognised flowering plants is the cowslip (*Primula veris*). In Ireland, this beautiful wild flower has not suffered near extinction by human avarice as have its fellows in the more densely populated parts of Great Britain, where it is now a rare native. The grasslands

and roadsides of the Irish midlands still support countless cowslips whose honeyed perfume adds to the wonderful, invigorating freshness of a soft spring breeze. Later in the summer the dusky pink blooms of marjoram (*Origanum vulgare*) will appear on dry grassy banks. When its leaves are bruised they emit the warm spicy smell so evocative of delicious Mediterranean cuisine.

Recently there have been considerable changes to the rural Irish landscape. Modernisation of the road system has given rise to some species-rich and visually attractive grasslands. The soil used to level the wide verges and embankments of these new roads is often poor in nutrients, thus artificially creating the conditions of an old hay meadow. With unusual wisdom, the many County Councils do not cut the grass until late in the summer, again mimicking the hay meadow regime. Seedlings of sycamore and ash, soon to be cut down by the council mowers, hint at the fate of these young grasslands if they were not mown each year. The roadside verges are often rich in common grasses which may have little agricultural value but are of considerable botanical interest. For example, the false oat-grass (*Arrhenatherum elatius*) resembles a fine cultivated oat plant and its big, strong stems and graceful flowers are beautiful in early July, especially when contrasted with the delicate flowers of the commoner species of

Bee orchid

Heath spotted orchid

Green-winged orchid

Frog orchid

ORCHIDS

Orchids belong to a huge plant family with 735 genera and some 17,000 species. The orchid family (Orchidaceae) belongs to the Monocotyledons along with the grasses, sedges, lilies and irises. Most of the orchid species are tropical. The orchids native to Ireland do not have the large showy flowers of some of their tropical cousins, but when seen close-up the flowers are no less amazing in their intricate detail. Many of the native orchids have fragile, fleshy rhizomes that will not tolerate disturbance of the soil. Orchid seed is among the smallest in the plant kingdom.

Twayblade

*Heath spotted orchids on
a grazed grassland on
shallow blanket peat.*

may also grow the commoner spotted orchids (*Dactylorhiza maculata* group) and green-flowered twayblade (*Listera ovata*) with its twin basal leaves giving the plant its common name.

The orchids are prized for their beauty, but the members of the large family to which the daisies and thistles belong are rarely treasured. The ribbons of vibrant yellow dandelions (*Taraxacum*) along the roads of the eastern areas in spring would be considered a more glorious sight if we did not despise the humble dandelion so much as a garden weed (see Chapter 8). Throughout the British Isles, all yellow daisy-like flowers are lumped together as dandelions but a little closer inspection will show that there are many yellow 'daisies' growing by the roadside edges which do not resemble the dandelion, save for having yellow flowers. There are many species of Compositae, for that is the family to which the daisies and thistles belong, which are notable for their variety of form. Some are small like the limey-yellow flowered, hairy, silver-leaved cat's ear (*Hypochoeris radicata*) which hugs the ground at the roadside edge. Other taller members of the family, like the species of milk- or sow-thistle (*Sonchus* species) flower in summer and have unmistakable thistle-like heads resembling small golden dish mops. The purple thistles (*Cirsium* species) which are in flower at the same time have very spiky, silvery leaves of great complexity

bent-grasses (*Agrostis* species), meadow grasses (*Poa* species) and the stiffer stems of ryegrass.

Amongst these beautiful grasses will be found some of our choicest orchids and none is more distinctive than the fragrant orchid (*Gymnadenia conopsea*). This most beautiful of flowers has the added attraction of a wonderful subtle and seductive perfume. Considering that the Irish flora has so few species which have fragrant flowers, for beauty of form and fragrance, *Gymnadenia* is almost unique. With the fragrant orchid

Cow parsley in early summer, replaces the yellow bands of dandelion that adorned these roadsides earlier in the season.

By mid summer the cow parsley is in seed and the hogweed takes its place.

Marjoram gives a Mediterranean look, and smell, to an Irish roadside.

and each topped with the brush of purple which is its complex flower head. In late summer the thistles, along with ragwort, are the most conspicuous flowers of the Irish roadside.

The golden 'dandelions' of autumn are not species of the genus *Taraxacum*, but belong to the genus *Leontodon* with autumnal hawkbit (*Leontodon autumnalis*) flowering in profusion in late September and joining the reds and blacks of the autumn hedgerow fruits. Throughout the year, even in the darkest days of winter, one or two species of the Compositae may be found flowering in some sheltered spot by the roadside. The small flowers of the groundsel (*Senecio vulgaris*) may survive a hard frost in a sheltered place and their insignificant flowers add specks of brightness to an otherwise bleak, bleached winter landscape, while the first pale pink flowers of its relative, the sweetly-scented winter heliotrope (*Petasites fragrans*), herald the arrival of spring.

In the late spring, as the flowers of the true dandelions fade from yellow to silvery fluffy seeds, they are replaced by the cow parsley or Queen Anne's lace (*Anthriscus sylvestris*) with its frothy white flowers on top of metre-high stalks. These common flowers make a bright, clean display beneath the unfurling green leaves of the woody hedge species. Where the hedge is of hawthorn, the contrast of this shrub's greenest of leaves with the creamy white of the cow parsley makes the lanes of Ireland look freshly laundered. Later in the season the coarser leaves and creamier flowers of the hogweed (*Heracleum sphondylium*) take the place of the cow parsley. Both these plants are members of the carrot family, Umbelliferae, which, with the Compositae, are well represented in the dry grassland which borders many Irish rural roads and lanes.

Betwixt and between the larger summer flowers and stiff stems of the grasses, scramble the lax-stemmed plants of the pea family, especially the vetches which are in the genus *Vicia*. The vetches and their near relative, the yellow-flowered meadow vetchling (*Lathyrus pratensis*), are common throughout most of the country. The vetches look like small versions of the sweet pea of garden cultivation, but with less colourful flowers and lacking the

Winter heliotrope flowers in late winter and early spring long before its large leaves have fully expanded.

powerful perfume of their cultivated relatives. Tufted vetch (*Vicia cracca*) has a long inflorescence of bright purple flowers while the flowers of bush vetch (*Vicia sepium*) are in more open heads and look dingy in comparison of those of their close relative.

Limestone grassland

Efforts are now being made to protect the most species-rich grasslands, including the limestone grasslands of the west of which those in counties Fermanagh and Leitrim are fine examples. The geology of Fermanagh is extremely complex and the various

Roadside stripped of topsoil, leaving the impoverished subsoil that allows many of the grassland herbs to compete against the grasses. Too rich a soil will allow the grasses to grow strongly and swamp the herbs.

Mature species-rich grassland developed on roadsides like that shown above.

vegetation systems best suited to the underlying soils form a patchwork of green limestone grassland and brown peatlands. So species-rich are these limestone grasslands that in spring or summer it is possible to identify almost twenty different plant species in an area no larger than the palm of a hand. Not all will be in flower but many have distinctive and readily distinguishable leaves. The fun of discovering this richness of plant life is that no prior botanical knowledge is necessary. Just count the different types of leaves and see how many you get.

In the short turf, the common and widespread grasses like the fescues (*Festuca* species) grow alongside the rare blue moor-grass (*Sesleria albicans*) which is restricted to limestone soils. Tiny violets (*Viola* species), perennial flax (*Linum perenne*), lady's bedstraw (*Galium verum*), harebell (*Campanula rotundifolia*) and birdsfoot-trefoil (*Lotus cornicularus*) form a living carpet richer in species than any of the blossom-strewn tapestries of the medieval French chateaux. Children love the bright egg-yolk-yellow flowers of the birdsfoot-trefoil, but farmers may love them more. Birdsfoot-trefoil is a widespread legume occurring in many grassland types, but is especially valuable in the upland limestone pastures where it provides good food for sheep. The short turf of these limestone grasslands is maintained by the hardy sheep which live on them all year round as the turf species can withstand the trampling and cutting of sharp sheep hooves.

The wealth of species growing on the limestone soils is in contrast to the relatively species-poor grasslands of the acidic soils. The grass species of the acidic upland soils commonly have narrow, bristly, less palatable leaves. Although most of the meadow grasses are absent from these acid grasslands, the almost ubiquitous sweet vernal-grass may be present, but invasion by mat-grass (*Nardus stricta*) will occur if grazing is diminished and conditions are

Bluebells grow almost to the high-tide mark in this exposed dry seaside grassland.

wet. The grassland dominated by mat-grass is a conspicuous feature of many eastern and northern hills, for example, the Mournes and the Sperrins. Mat-grass dominated grasslands develop on flat or gently rolling sloping areas on the summits or shoulders of hills. Mat-grass has a much-branched, tough, horizontally-growing rhizome almost on the soil surface. This sends up leafy and flowering shoots which are enclosed by thick, tough, basal sheaths which persist long after the leaves are dead and fallen. The tough rhizomes and sheaths slowly decay and form a peaty layer further colonised by mat-grass. Another tussock-forming grass, the wavy hair-grass (*Deschampsia flexuosa*) will also thrive on the peaty humus formed under mat-grass, where the hair-grass tussock bases are slow to rot and continue to accumulate acidic humus long after the leaf bases have died.

A third common upland grass is the purple moor-grass. The bluish-leaved moor-grass has many characteristics in common with mat-grass but needs more water so it occurs freely in many types of wet peaty soils where it forms a very muddy humus. Its leaves are long and narrow but flat, not bristly like those of mat-grass, therefore it may form tussocks or a more lawn-like meadow.

These nutrient-poor upland grasslands have been formed and are maintained by grazing pressure. But even the hardy sheep of the Irish uplands find a thin living on the wetter,

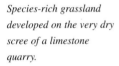

Species-rich grassland developed on the very dry scree of a limestone quarry.

acidic grasslands which degenerate into
upland peats if grazing pressure is
reduced. On the higher or wetter slopes
this grazing belt may be replaced by bog
and in the wet west this bog may
encroach down to sea level.

5 LIMESTONE

The underlying rock of large areas of Ireland is Carboniferous limestone (see map on page 2) formed 340 million years ago, but over central Ireland this rock is largely covered by a blanket of later glacial clays and gravels. It is only in areas where the ice has scraped the limestone clean that the limestone karst landscape and its characteristic flora has developed. The karst landscape develops because the limestone dissolves very slowly in rainwater. The water widens the natural cracks in the limestone and eventually forms huge cave systems underground. The cracks follow lines of weakness in the rock which open up to provide a home for plants in an otherwise barren and hostile environment.

The most famous of these karst areas in Ireland is the Burren in County Clare. Here some 250 square kilometres of karst landscape, limestone hills and shoreline form a famous botanical area which no book on Irish plants could ignore. There are, however, already several authoritative books, numerous small guides and journal articles about the Burren. This chapter in no way provides a substitute to these works, but rather tries to give a flavour of the area, discusses what is known of its vegetational history and puts it in the context of other limestone areas in Ireland.

The unique landscape of the Burren deserves a special visit, unlike the grasslands and sea shore which may be appreciated in all parts of Ireland. Even during a brief visit, there is much in the

Species-rich limestone grassland with fragrant orchids in the uplands of the Burren.

*Characteristic view of the coastal part of the Burren with a mixture
of bare limestone and grassland.*

Close up view of the grassland.

Burren for the visitor to appreciate. Any visit should try to include three main areas, the coastal strip, the flat limestone 'pavement' and the hill tops. Each of these has a distinctive landscape and range of plants. Robert Lloyd Praeger, (1947 - *The Way That I Went* - still essential reading before botanical expeditions in Ireland) recommended starting a visit to the Burren at the coast near Black Head. The coast road here is much improved from his day and provides an ideal circuit of the area and the sand dunes at Fanad are also worth a visit.

Where the Burren limestone meets the sea, seaside plants mingle with limestone plants. One of the special summer delights here is the mixture of the bright crimson of the lime-loving bloody crane's-bill (*Geranium sanguineum*), the pink of thrift (*Armeria maritima*) and the pale creams of sea campion (*Silene vulgaris* subspecies *maritima*) and burnet rose (*Rosa pimpinellifolia*). The coast road runs along a shelf; actually the level of the beach in former times of higher sea level. Just above the road there are steep slopes which were once the sea cliff and

Thrift and bloody cranes-bill on the limestone ledges above the sea.

Spring gentians. (Photo: R. Govier.)   *Herb-Robert.*

Spring gentians.

here the real Burren flora can be appreciated. The white flowers of the mountain avens blanket these hillsides for a brief spell in May, to be replaced by the tufts of seed heads each neatly rolled into a spiral until they are ready to shed their seeds later in the summer. Scattered amongst the mountain avens

are another of the special joys of the Burren, the spring gentian (*Gentiana verna*). No photograph can do justice to the luminous blue of this flower. The spring gentian is known in alpine areas in the rest of Europe as far as arctic Russia, always above 460m. Only in Ireland is it found almost to sea level. It is still a puzzle that so many Arctic plants are found here so close to sea level whereas elsewhere in Europe they are mostly found only at high altitudes as, for example, in the Cairngorms in Scotland and Teesdale in the north of England.

Most of the other plants typical of limestone may also be seen on these slopes near the road, but on the higher ground more of the Arctic nature of this vegetation becomes apparent. Here saxifrages and juniper, along with the mountain avens and sheets of the hoary

Mountain avens. Early flowering plants usually have eight petals as suggested by the Latin species name octapetala, *but later-flowering plants often have double or semi-double flowers. (Photo: R. Govier.)*

rock-rose (*Helianthemum canum*) suggest a similar scene 11,000 years ago when Arctic plants first spread back over the area after the retreat of the ice. Around Black Head, the big rounded boulders that were moved here by the ice of the last glaciation provide further proof that this area was glaciated.

The next place to visit is the flat limestone pavement. There are large areas of pavement on the higher ground and also on the eastern margins of the Burren. Where the ground is very exposed to the westerly winds and where the limestone is hard, there is little vegetation on the flat surfaces, but look closer and you will see the plants hiding in the cracks and in the dips and hollows in the limestone. In the cracks there is a profusion of ferns peculiar to limestone, together with more ubiquitous ferns such as the strap-like hart's-tongue fern (*Asplenium scolopendrium*) which is also common in woodlands. The ferns of limestone soils were once restricted to areas such as the Burren, but are now found over much of Ireland growing in the lime-rich mortar of stone walls. The rustyback fern (*Asplenium ceterach*), the little wall-rue (*Asplenium ruta-muraria*) and the maidenhair spleenwort (*Asplenium trichomanes*) can all be found in stone walls in areas far from any local limestone.

The limestone seems completely treeless, but there are holly, ash, hawthorn, blackthorn, hazel, spindle, guelder rose and others, all growing in

Hart's-tongue fern in cracks in the limestone.

cracks with their heads below the surface of the wind-torn pavement. These trees live with their roots in the cracks where small pockets of 'humus' – the dark peaty material formed from decayed plant remains – retain moisture. Their twigs reach up from the dark depths of the crack to the light, but are cut off by wind

The rustyback fern, one of the ferns that has adapted well to life on stone walls throughout Ireland.

Several of the orchids
common in the Burren:

O'Kelly's orchid (left).
Fragrant orchid (right).

Spotted orchid (left).
Pyramidal orchid (right).

Common speedwell, one of
the short grassland plants
(left).
Burnet rose, common on
the rougher limestone
areas (right).

Holly tree on a limestone pavement (left).
Stone bramble, a relative of the blackberry (right).

Spindle (left).
Ash tree growing within a limestone crack (right).

Elder on the less windswept eastern side of the Burren (left).
Herd of goats grazing on the high ground of the Burren (right).

Mountain everlasting, a typical plant of the short limestone grassland.

The blue-flowered milkwort.

with a few rocks to almost bare limestone. Here grow, together with the mountain avens, some of the smaller plants such as saxifrages, mountain everlasting (*Antennaria dioica*) with its silver-backed leaves, the common speedwell (*Veronica persica*) and the blue-flowered common milkwort (*Polygala vulgaris*). The milkwort is found in short grass all over Ireland and, while it is usually blue, it can also be found in a range of shades through to pink and white.

It is in the short grassland in the less rocky areas that the orchids of the Burren abound. Commonest are the early purple orchid, pyramidal orchid, fragrant orchid and the common spotted orchid, with its white-flowered form known as O'Kelly's orchid (*Dactylorhiza fuchsii* subspecies *okellyi*). With these may be found the twayblade and a more diligent search will reveal many of the rarer orchids for which this area is famous. There are also some of the more familiar woodland plants like primrose and wood sage (*Teucrium scorodonia*), which seem out of context in this harsh environment.

In a few areas there are extensive patches of hazel woodland on the flat limestone and many of the steep valley sides also have a covering of hazel and ash. This is the nearest we can get to an image of what most of Ireland looked like during the hazel phase of the early post glacial some 9,000 years ago. The hazel is cut back each year by the salt

and grazing animals to produce natural 'bonsai' trees. Wind is not the only factor in keeping the vegetation at a low level. Most of the Burren is grazed by sheep and rabbits and there is also a population of feral goats that live on the higher ground. The limestone pavement of the central area ranges from dry grassland

The alien red valerian forming a dramatic patch of colour on rough limestone pavement.

Juniper with fruit.

The prostrate form of juniper.

An upright form of juniper showing the effect of strong winds.

winds of winter or spring. All the more exposed bushes have dead twigs protruding above the general level of the canopy. Much of the hazel woodland is grazed by cattle and the ground vegetation is very trampled, but primrose, wood sage and herb Robert (*Geranium robertianum*) thrive.

On the north-eastern fringe of the Burren there is an extensive flat area with rather more small trees and shrubs. Here juniper is more abundant and more frequently fruiting. There are also a few upright junipers. These appear to be a

View over the Burren showing peat-covered limestone at high altitude in the foreground, bare limestone pavement in the middle distance and a steep-sided valley with hazel woodland leading to the sea.

different variety or type of juniper as they grow alongside the more usual prostrate form. Near the northern edge of the Burren, the invasion of aliens such as sycamore and the startlingly bright red valerian (*Centranthus ruber*) are increasingly common.

The third area to visit is the hill tops. These are interesting, apart from the stunning views, as much of the limestone is covered by a thin and patchy peat covering. This leads to the interesting juxtaposition of the alkaline lime-loving plants with the plants of acid bogland. Ling is common growing alongside bloody crane's-bill.

Turloughs

A feature of limestone areas is variability of lake-water levels. Lakes connected to the underground water systems in the limestone can fill with water in winter and empty completely in the summer. These seasonal lakes, called turloughs, have a characteristic flora that can tolerate being immersed in water for as much as six months of the year.

Visitors to the Burren in winter will see a landscape devoid of the bright colours which are such a striking feature of the early summer, but a walk on the limestone may reveal plants easily overlooked in the warmer months. Few of the Burren's herbaceous plants are evergreen but the wild madder (*Rubia peregrina*) with its straggling stems and coarse, dark green, leaves may be found amongst bare branches of stunted blackthorn. A little inland, rue-leaved saxifrage, which can tolerate extremes of dryness in summer, can be found as tiny overwintering rosettes of leaves growing on the thin humus in hollows in the limestone, which at this time of year are completely waterlogged.

The history of the Burren

The plant history of the Burren, as with

most of the vegetational history told in this book, comes from pollen analysis. The problem in the Burren is finding deposits that preserve pollen. There are no deep bogs and many of the lakes are turloughs in which the seasonal drying destroys the pollen. The history of the Burren has been pieced together from analysis of deposits from a number of small lakes mainly in the south east of the area. It is clear that the greater part of the Burren was wooded through most of the post-glacial. This region went through the same vegetational stages as the rest of Ireland (see Chapter 1) with an initial colonisation by Arctic plants, then birch woodland, giving way to hazel woodland, then a mixed forest, but with a greater predominance of pine than elsewhere in Ireland, especially on the higher ground. The destruction of the forest starts here,

The deep cracks in the limestone provide shelter and refuge from grazing for a wide range of plants, from trees to ferns and mosses.

as elsewhere in Ireland, some 6,000 years ago. Shortly after this the yew tree appears, contributing substantially to the

Dovedale moss or mossy saxifrage, one of the mat-forming saxifrages.

Irish saxifrage, found only in western counties of Ireland and north-west and central Europe.

total pollen which is interpreted as representing considerable stands of yew woodland, much as can be seen in Killarney today. Yew can now be found in or on the limestone pavement and on steep cliffs, but only as infrequent, low, stunted bushes.

Following the first farming 6,000 years ago there was continual, if fluctuating, human settlement in the area and stone structures, some burial, some domestic and some defensive may be seen from all archaeological periods.

The significant difference between the Burren and most of the rest of Ireland is that there must have been

some areas of sufficiently thin tree cover right through the last 10,000 years to have allowed the Arctic component of the vegetation to survive. Having said that, pollen of most of the Arctic/alpine plants is completely missing in the pollen record for the period between the end of the ice age and the last few hundred years. Pollen of the mountain avens is common at the end of the glacial period, but is completely absent even from sites where the plant is now abundant. We must presume that during the time of maximum forest cover the Arctic/alpine plants managed to survive on a few exposed cliffs and mountain

*Hairy rock-cress (*Arabis hirsuta*), abundant on the limestone pavement.*

The bristly leaves of wild madder. Its cultivated relative was an important plant in medieval times as it is one of the few plants that produce a red dye. (Photo: R. Govier.)

Hoary rock-rose.

Shrubby cinquefoil.

tops whereas in most of Ireland they were completely eliminated by the dense forest cover. Wherever the special flora of the Burren survived during the post-glacial it was significantly less abundant than it is now. The Burren, then, must be seen as another part of the Irish landscape that owes its present floristic diversity to the activities of forest clearance for farming.

Other limestone areas

There are no areas of limestone in Ireland where the typical 'pavement' is so well developed as in the Burren. Comparable areas in England may be seen in the Malham Tarn area in Yorkshire, and the relatively small limestone region in Fermanagh has some limestone pavement with many of the characteristic plants such as mountain avens, juniper and mossy saxifrage, but the area is only a few square kilometres in extent.

Much of the rest of the limestone of central Ireland is covered by boulder clay left by successive glaciations. This rich land was densely forested in earlier times and intensively farmed more recently, providing no habitat for the Arctic component. The much younger Tertiary limestone of the north east of Ireland is more like the chalk of the Downs of the south of England and is too soft for karst features to form. A few lime-loving plants, however, may be found on the chalk screes of the Antrim coast.

Hazel wood and limestone grassland both probably maintained in their present form by grazing.

Chalk-raised beach on the Antrim coast is home to some lime-loving plants.

Several plants of the limestone areas of Ireland also find favour as garden plants.

Bloody cranesbill.

Water avens.

6 SEA SHORE

The summer visitor to the soft and friendly holiday beaches of Portrush in County Antrim and Ballybunion in County Kerry sees the gentle face of our varied coastline. A visit to those places during a January gale, when the sand-laden wind stings the skin, is in startling contrast to the bright calm days of summer. The cries of thousands of seabirds over the Blasket Islands cannot compete in volume with the howling wind and thunderous crashing of the waves in those same places in mid-March.

Sandy beaches are only one of the many types of habitat on Ireland's long and varied coastline. At one extreme are soaring cliffs such as the Cliffs of Moher in County Clare, the high, steep, rocky edges around the Giant's Causeway in County Antrim and Malin Head in County Donegal. While at the other extreme there are quiet waters, sheltered from the erosional effects of the waves, which lap the edges of the muddy or peaty coasts of Mill Bay in

On a more sheltered shore, the sea aster thrives in the decomposing seaweed of a strand line.

The bright sea pink contrasts with the orange of the lichen (Zanthoria species) on this exposed rocky shore.

County Down or Mulrany in County Mayo, allowing flat, low-lying salt marshes to develop. Between these extremes are the sand dunes or beaches of shingle and pebbles. All of these places support plants which may be either specific to one particular habitat or may be discovered growing in more than one of these salty environments, as well as in other places beyond the influence of the salt-laden winds and tides.

The plants best adapted to live on the coasts are those that can tolerate salt, with many also having strategies geared to conserving their internal fresh water. There are only about twenty species in Ireland that can tolerate this hostile environment. High concentrations of salt can play havoc with a plant's ability to regulate its chemistry. In the concentrations of salt found in sea water, plant cells desiccate, so it is not surprising that some plants of the Irish coasts have the same characteristics as desert plants – they have the capacity to retain water and are thus known as xerophytes, meaning 'plants of dry places'. In addition, many also have mechanisms to rid their cells of excess salt. It is worth noting that Ireland has no salt-tolerant trees, therefore we do not have habitats like the mangrove swamps of the tropical regions.

Species like the sea lavender (*Limonium humile*), which commonly grows on the permanently-damp muds of the salt marsh, have juicy leaves which retain cell sap and secretory glands on their leaf surfaces to expel excess salt. These plants are regularly covered by the incoming tide and for part of their daily lives thrive in conditions which are otherwise the

Lax-flowered sea lavender grows on salt marshes and occasionally as a strand-line plant on sheltered shores.

The succulent-leaved seablite has many of the characteristics of a desert plant.

domain of the seaweeds. In Ireland, sea lavender is often found growing with another salt marsh species, the annual seablite (*Suaeda maritima*).

On the extremely dry sand dunes, where salt-laden winds could dry plant tissues, the grasses employ a different mechanism to conserve their inner sap. Their leaves have internal structures to reduce water loss. All leaves of flowering plants are peppered with microscopic pores or *stomata* which allow the plant to exchange gases with the atmosphere; but where air can leave the plants so also can water vapour be lost. To reduce the amount of water lost as vapour to the drying winds of the coasts, many grasses such as marram grass (*Ammophila arenaria*) have leaves which bear stomata only in the grooves between the leaf ribs on the lower surface. When the air is dry, the leaves roll to enclose the stomata on the inside and thus reduce water loss. The leaves also have short hairs which line the grooves forming a further barrier to desiccation.

In addition to coping with salt, those plants which grow on the unstable edges of mud flats, salt-marshes and sand dunes must also be able to grow on substrates which are constantly moving.

Marram grass dominates the shifting sands of young sand dunes. In wet weather the leaf blade is flat, but in dry conditions the leaf is tightly rolled to conserve moisture.

Indeed, it is their ability to germinate and grow under these conditions which enables them to trap and eventually stabilise these constantly shifting substrates. For example, marram grass, common on sandy beaches where high mounds or sand dunes have formed, can tolerate burial by up to a metre of sand a year. Individual plants or 'genets' of marram may reach an age of hundreds of years. Various different types of plants, each with an internal body chemistry adapted to life on the coasts, will therefore stabilise both the dry, drifting sands of the dunes and watery, mobile muds of the salt marshes.

A few Irish native flowering plants are as well adapted to life in the sea as the seaweeds. There are three species of marine flowering plants known as eelgrass (*Zostera* species) found in Ireland. All have grass-like foliage and all three species grow in the shallows of mudflats with *Z. marina*, the species best adapted to an aquatic existence, spending all of its life immersed in sea water. The eelgrasses are the first of the mud-binders and, with some species of filamentous green algae, begin the processes which can eventually turn parts of the sea bed into dry land. Eelgrass is an important food plant of wildfowl which suffered badly in the 1930s when eelgrass beds throughout Ireland and Great Britian were all but wiped out by a wasting disease. Not all eelgrass species were equally affected, but many years elapsed before the beds returned to their previous luxuriance. Today the eelgrass beds around Ireland's coast provide food for thousands of over-wintering waterfowl, either directly or as a habitat for a range of invertebrate animals eaten by the birds. Huge numbers of brent geese live on Strangford Lough in County Down during the winter months when the eelgrass beds provide them with vital nourishment.

Extensive beds of the eelgrass colonise these mud flats in Strangford Lough and provide food for flocks of brent geese. The Lough is marine and the eelgrass is under water for about half of each day.

Salt marsh plants

Mud flats and salt marshes are less well-known than the sandy or shingly beaches but the plants of the muddy shores are well worthy of discovery. To fully appreciate the salt-marsh plants

The glassworts are amongst the first colonisers of bare mud.

A network of channels bring sea water to this salt marsh twice a day. The higher parts remain dry enough for grazing except during spring tides.

and the wide range of conditions they experience, visit a salt-marsh in summer and stay on or near the marsh for a full cycle of the tide. Watch the slow ebb of the water and see the newly-exposed bluish-green grassy sward, peppered purple and pink with flowers. These highly specialised flowering plants are able to thrive in sea water while being rocked by the tide for hours on end.

Salt marshes are flat and wet and made up of material previously eroded from the land or sea bed. They may develop on sand, shingle or even on the peaty-silts at the edges of the lowland Atlantic bogs on the west Irish coast. As the sediments which make the salt marsh can settle only in fairly still water, they

form in relatively sheltered inlets, where broad expanses of tidal flats or coastal spits dissipate wave energy, where the rise and fall of the tide is gentle and where waves are low and exert little force in their downward plunge. If all of these conditions prevail, sediment is deposited and not washed away by the next tide. Eventually the level of the deposited sediment rises sufficiently to create land which is dry for part of each day. Therein lies the secret of the start of a salt-marsh.

The next phase of marsh development depends on one or two species of colonising plants, because without their mud-binding properties, the marsh will not continue to develop. Only

native plants are the annual glassworts (*Salicornia* species). These remarkable plants live most of the day rooted in mud almost devoid of oxygen and in slightly turbid water where light conditions are poor. The shape and chemistry of the plant enables it to grow and flower despite daily duress. The succulent leaf bases conceal the stem with the inconspicuous flowers hidden within the plant. The seeds are usually dispersed only when the plant dies and decays during the winter. The following year the seeds germinate in the mud where they fell. Due to their unique anatomy, the glassworts present botanists with difficulties when attempting to separate species. In the 1999 edition of *An Irish Flora*, the authors emphasise the species'

Sea arrow grass.

The invasive cord-grass is expanding in many Irish coastal sites.

a few species can withstand conditions at the leading edge of the marsh where they are submerged in slightly muddy, lapping sea water for part of each day and exposed to bright light and the drying effects of the air for the remainder. The best adapted of these

apparently distinct local variants and remind readers that 'even now there is still much to be learnt about Irish plants'.

Just to the landward side of the glasswort zone is the domain of the seablite. This bluish-green annual continues to bind sediment and may now be joined by others which also thrive in the very wet but open conditions near the edge of the marsh.

Until this century the glasswort and seablite were the plants most likely to be found at the leading edge of salt-marshes throughout Ireland and Great Britian, but this is no longer the case. The most mobile areas of numerous mudflats not previously colonized by flowering plants now support swiftly-expanding stands of a hybrid cord grass, *Spartina* x *townsendii*. This hybrid is the result of a mating between *S. alterniflora*, an alien species naturalised in Great Britain and the British native *S. maritima*; neither species is native to Ireland. *Spartina alterniflora* was first recorded in England in 1829 and the hybrid was first seen in Poole Harbour in Dorset. It is an extraordinarily efficient mud binder, and was introduced by railway companies to a number of locations in Ireland in the late 1920s and 1930s to stabilise mud flats on the seaward side of railway

Sea aster is common both on salt marshes and on rocky shores.

Sea aster.

Rock samphire.

The shrubby sea purslane is the only native
woody coastal species in Ireland.

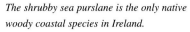

*The sea pink is naturally
variable in colour and has
given rise to many garden
cultivars. It is also well
known to those who
remember the pre-decimal
sterling currency as it was
portrayed on the reverse of
the threepenny coin.*

*Salt, spread on icy roads,
encourages the growth of
scurvy-grass.*

Scurvy-grass.

embankments, from where it has since
spread. Like glasswort, cord grass seeds
will germinate while submerged and
where water quality creates poor light
conditions, with cord-grass able to
survive prolonged periods of
submergence in water turbid with silt
and with little light available for
photosynthesis. Unfortunately, the
invasive cord grass hybrid and its fertile
derivative (*Spartina anglica*) are
becoming increasingly common in Irish
salt-marshes where they present a
growing threat to native biodiversity.

There is considerable variation from
marsh to marsh, especially in the strip

just landward of the first mud-binding plants. In this zone grow a mixture of species including the purple-flowered, succulent-leaved, sea aster (*Aster tripolium*) and the fine-leaved, common saltmarsh-grass (*Puccinellia maritima*). Less showy but in intimate mix with the grasses and sea aster will be found the sea plantain (*Plantago maritima*), sea-spurrey (*Spergularia species*) and sea arrowgrass (*Triglochin maritima*) with additional colour from the flowers of sea lavender and sea pink or thrift. Sea pink is also a plant of rocky shores and some mountain habitats in Ireland and Scotland. The pollen of sea pink is resistant to sea water, while the fruit may float buoyantly on the tide, adaptations fitting for a plant which grows well in maritime conditions.

Common scurvy-grass (*Cochlearia officinalis*) is one of the coastal plants which, like the sea pink, can grow as well on the rocky shores as it does on the salty muds. Common scurvy-grass has evergreen, thick leaves and produces small, clean, white flowers profusely in spring and intermittently throughout the summer and autumn months. Once restricted to the coasts, it now occupies a new habitat. Thin ribbons of scurvy grass line the central reservations of

This marram tussock shows dramatically how plants can trap sand and initiate dune building.

The distinctive flat, blue leaves of the sand couch-grass make it stand out from the surrounding marram grass.

The prickly saltwort grows on bare sand just above the high tide line.

The fleshy sea sandwort also traps sand on the beach edge.

motorways as here salt, scattered to prevent winter ice, has accumulated. The salty, exposed bases of the embankment are also windy places. In these artificial salty and windy places, so like the coastal cliffs and salt marshes, the scurvy grass does well.

In Ireland there is but one shrubby salt-marsh species, *Atriplex* (formerly *Halimione*) *portulacoides*, the sea purslane. Evidence from sites throughout the British Isles shows that the range of this plant has extended throughout the twentieth century, but the conditions which have favoured this expansion are not understood. As well as an expansion in range, the plant is now found throughout the tidal range of many marshes on the east Irish coast, though missing from those in the west. Its northern limit in Ireland is at Ballymacormick Point near Groomsport in north County Down.

As the marsh slopes upwards away from the sea so the upper reaches may be swamped by the tide only a few times a year. These upper parts of the marsh, submerged for the shortest time, may have little salt in the substrate because of

Frosted orache, one of several orache species common on sandy and stony Irish shores.

repeated dilution by rain. The back of the marsh supports additional common species like the sea rushes (*Juncus maritimus* and *J. gerardi*) with the sea beet (*Beta vulgaris* sub-species *maritima*), a widespread, native succulent related to the beet of cultivation. As the marsh blends with the surrounding land, non-marsh species, still relatively tolerant of salt, will grow. These include other species of rush and the common reed.

Some marshes provide good grazing for cattle and sheep, but their trampling affects the marsh, with some plants such as sea lavender less tolerant of this pressure than others while other marsh species are intolerant of pollution. Salt marshes close to urban and industrial centres have, in many cases, been obliterated by development or so damaged by pollution as to be unrecognisable. The status of the estuarine salt-marshes close to towns

should be monitored as these habitats are in decline in many areas of the British Isles. On a wider scale, as the effects of global warming and consequent sea level rise are becoming apparent, the fate of salt-marshes and other types of saline wetlands may be bleak. Despite

Sea campion.

Seakale is both a tough native seaside plant and a luxury vegetable.

The oyster plant, one of the rarest Irish coastal plants.

considerable research, there is still much to be learnt about the many factors which influence the maritime marsh flora.

Sandy beach plants

The greatest contrast between salt-marshes and one of the other major coastal habitats, sand dunes, occurs at the seaward edge of both systems. Whereas the edge of the salt marsh or mud flat is constantly wet, the edge of a dune system represents possibly the driest natural environment in Ireland. In these dry places the plants which help to build and stabilise the dunes must be capable of surviving swift burial by blowing sand, the constant physiological stress of drying wind and an erratic supply of fresh water.

There is considerable regional variation in the species which first colonise the bare and mobile sands of Irish beaches and it is plants adapted to these harsh conditions which first trap the dry, shifting grains of sand. The tiny mounds which form at the base of the specialised sea-shore grasses will, in time, form the nucleus of a sand dune which may ultimately attain many metres in height and extent. Sand couch-grass (*Elymus farctus*) has fibrous stems and leaves and is one of the first plants to stabilise sands because it can tolerate the mechanical damage caused by the winds which whip and swirl dry sand grains along an exposed beach.

On some sandy beaches the sand couch may be found growing close by another tough native. A walk on bare feet along the high tide line of some Irish strands can be very uncomfortable if the prickly saltwort (*Salsola kali*) grows in the sand. This prostrate annual spreads its prickle-ended leaves and swiftly traps and holds the sand grains seen drifting over the beach surface in a stiff breeze. Prickly saltwort, like the glasswort of the salt marsh, has succulent leaves and is tolerant of very salty conditions but it is found only in drier places. The skeletons of plants of years past continue to hold trapped sand and it is these which may cause pain to the feet of the unsuspecting beach comber.

The sea pea photographed in a seaside garden. This species is rare in the wild.

More common than prickly saltwort at the high tide area of some beaches is the spine-free, but thick and fleshy-leaved, perennial sea sandwort (*Honckenya peploides*). The low-growing sea sandwort is well adapted to stabilising both sands and gravels. The oraches (*Atriplex* species) are also to be found in abundance near the top of sandy, muddy or gravelly beaches. The perennial sea milkwort (*Glaux maritima*) is common on salt marshes where its lax stems straggle through the plants in the middle of the marsh but on some stony shores its

The sharp spines of the sea holly do not seem to deter snails from taking an early morning feed.

growth is not lax but squat and its small pink flowers are readily observed in June.

The sea sandwort may grow with sea campion (*Silene vulgaris* subspecies *maritima*) which has pure white petals protruding from a puffy net-veined pouch of sepals. Bladder campion has two well-defined subspecies of which *maritima* is common on rocky and shingly beaches throughout the country. The sea rocket (*Cakile maritima*) with its white flowers and thick, lobed leaves is yet another pretty annual well-suited to life on the exposed shores and, while relatively common in the north and east, it is rarer on the shores of the south and west.

There are a number of other seaside plants to be found along shingly shores, some locally common and at least one being a great rarity. The cultivated seakale (*Crambe maritima*) is a delicious vegetable which is also one of our rarest native plants. It is therefore commoner on the dinner plate than growing wild, where it may be restricted now to only two sites in Ireland and records show that it is decreasing throughout its British Isles range, possibly because of habitat loss. This seaside vegetable grows on shingle within the range of the sea spray and can survive occasional inundation by the sea. All parts of the plant are striking, in particular its heavy though buoyant seeds and thick leaves with their waxy, virtually unwettable coating. The oyster plant (*Mertensia maritima*) also grows on shingle and is almost as rare in Ireland as the seakale. It too has thick, grey-green leaves though these are small when compared with those of seakale. The bright blue to pink flowers of the oyster plant distinguish it from all other plants of the shoreline.

The sea pea (*Lathyrus japonicus* subspecies *maritimus*) is a rare perennial western coastal plant found on sand and shingle shores, with most Irish records from County Kerry. This distinctive

The wild pansy thrives on the dry sunny banks of sand dunes.

Thyme adds fragrance to the sand dune flora.

Restharrow stands out with its distinctive grey leaves and pink flowers.

Centaury on the drier parts of a dune slack.

member of the pea family sprawls over the surface of shingle and also has the blue-green foliage characteristic of so many coastal plants, with blue-purple or occasionally white flowers. It is classed as a native but many of the plants which grow and flower each year on western

Irish coasts are not the parents of future generations. Each year the native population is enhanced by newcomers. The small Irish populations are unable to produce the large number of seeds which germinate on Irish beaches, suggesting that several thousand cross the Atlantic.

The sea pea re-invades Ireland each year as its seeds are buoyant and cross the Atlantic from North America where it is common. These buoyant seeds are stranded on the high shores of Kerry and the adjacent coasts following strong west and south-westerly storms with most

The autumn lady's tresses is hard to see except when the distinct spirally arranged flowers are present.

The pink flowers and twining thread-like stems belong to the parasitic dodder.

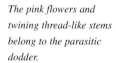

The white flowers of the grass of Parnassus adorn the wetter parts of a dune slack behind the main sand dunes at Mullaghmore in County Sligo.

The dome shape of the wild carrot flower distinguish it from other members of the family. The leaves smell strongly of carrot.

plants growing on beaches re-worked by storm events. Extra weight is added to the argument for re-invasion from the west as sea pea is not found on the eastern coasts of Ireland.

The sea holly (*Eryngium maritimum*) is a native plant of great architectural beauty which has caught the eye of the horticulturalist, therefore there are many varieties in garden cultivation. In Ireland the wild plant, however, grows on some sandy shores where it may be reasonably frequent, whereas populations are in decline in Scotland. It is every bit as spiky as its name suggests but unlike true holly the leaves are pale bluish-grey and the pale blue flowers are interspersed amongst prickly, modified leaves or bracts.

Sand dunes

Many species of herbaceous plants such as the wild pansy (*Viola tricolor*) contribute to the mosaic of floral colour which spangles the dunes with the passing of the seasons. In Ireland pink-flowered native plants are uncommon but many sand dunes support

Mayweed is at home on the coast as well as inland.

The sea beet flowers in its second year, like cultivated beetroot.

Wild radish.

The wild radish also forms a compact rosette in the first year and sends up a tall flowering spike in the second year.

The seedpods of wild radish.

common centaury (*Centaurium erythraea*) and the low, creeping, pea-flowered restharrow (*Ononis repens*) most frequent in the south and east. Wild thyme (*Thymus praecox*) has pinkish-purple flowers and its bruised leaves emit its characteristic fragrance. On some dunes during autumn, the rusty-red stems of dodder (*Cuscuta epithymum*) scramble through and between the stems of the dune grasses. Dodder is one of the few Irish plants which is completely parasitic.

Many common plants of dunes are not restricted to the sand dune habitat; some members of the daisy family such as ragwort (*Senecio jacobaea*), coltsfoot (*Tussilago farfara*) and groundsel are even more common in cultivated fields or on the waysides. Plants commonly thought to be restricted to fields such as silverweed (*Potentilla anserina*) are also found on some dune systems.

There is often a damp area trapped behind or within sand dunes that is termed a dune slack. These slacks are usually grazed by rabbits and have the flora of a species-rich grassland. One of the most famous is the dune slack at Mullaghmore in County Sligo which now has the status of a National Heritage Area. This area grades from dry, species-rich grassland, through a damp grassland with water mint (*Mentha aquatica*), rushes, reeds and iris into an area that is flooded for most of the year. Later in the year part of the slack is smothered in the white blossoms of the grass of Parnassus (*Parnassia palustris*). This beautiful white-flowered plant may be abundant in damp dune slacks but it is by no means universal. An expanse of flowering grass of Parnassus is a memorable sight. As autumn draws on there appears possibly the last of the native orchids to flower, the autumn lady's tresses (*Spiranthes spiralis*) which has its small, white flowers spiralling round the upper part of the stem of the plant, giving rise to its specific Latin name.

Silverweed, our only silver-leaved, yellow-flowered native.

Scentless mayweed.

Other dune systems, without a slack area, grade into heath. The fresh sand near the beach has a proportion of lime-rich ground shell, making the sand moderately alkaline. With age, the calcium carbonate leaches out leaving the sand in the older dunes acidic. The old dunes are likely to be colonised by acid-tolerant plants such as bell heather and ling and also the invasive fern, bracken (*Pteridium aquilinum*). Old dunes of this type are also likely to be invaded by non-native trees such as sycamore and the salt-tolerant maritime pine (*Pinus pinaster*).

Shingle beach plants

Those coasts that are not sandy or muddy are usually stony. These are actually the shorelines most often seen because the stretches of raised beach (see Chapter 1) used for coastal roads in

Sea spurrey flowering just above high tide line on a rocky shore.

The rich mixed flora of the dune slack at Mullaghmore, County Sligo.

most of the northern half of Ireland produce shingle beaches. Here the mud and sand building plants are not so common but many of the primitive ancestors of our cultivated vegetables grow. The sea beet, ancestor of the sugar beet, beetroot, spinach beet, chard and mangold, grows with the wild carrot (*Daucus carota*) and the wild radish (*Raphanus raphanistrum*). All three of these biennial plants lay down reserves in their roots in their first year of growth and produce flowers and seeds in their second year. It is these overwintering reserves in the beet, carrot and radish that were discovered and improved to produce the modern vegetables. They are also plants of disturbed and shifting soils making them ideal for the disturbed ground of field and garden.

These shingle shores were also probably the natural home of many garden weeds. Plants of disturbed ground such as the silverweed and the scentless mayweed (*Tripleurospernum inodorum* and *T. maritimum*) and other garden weeds such as couch-grass (*Elymus repens*) and ragwort may have had their home by the sea before being provided with more congenial surroundings by humans.

7 THE LANDSCAPE DIVIDED: HEDGES

An air traveller looking out of the window on the approach to landing at an Irish airport may be struck by the hundreds of small, irregularly-shaped fields. The average farm size in Ireland is much smaller than in most of Europe with over half of the farms less than twenty hectares. In summer, this picture is most colourful as the landscape appears covered by a huge patchwork quilt. The small, green fields of the pastures, interspersed with the golden hues of the ripening barley, oats and wheat, are all stitched together by the darker green lines of the hedges. The uplands too have a patchwork-like appearance but here each 'patch' may be edged with grey, not green, as instead of hedges there are dry-stone walls.

Enclosure is an amalgam of territorial delineation and the need to parcel the countryside into manageable areas for farming. The walls and hedges separate individual farms or holdings and are essential for stock control or crop management but enclosure and demarcation are no longer restricted to

Ancient field walls under blanket peat at Ceide in north County Mayo.

Aerial view of a drumlin landscape with a patchwork of fields divided by hedges.

the countryside. In the modern town, the practice lives on as minute land holdings, characterised by the gardens of semi-detached houses, are often bounded and separated from their neighbours and the pavement by lines of sombre green privet.

Something is known of the history of enclosure in Ireland from archaeology, pollen analysis and historical documentary records. The first walls are almost as old as the first signs of agriculture in the Irish pollen analytical record, for, at Ceide in north County Mayo, on the edge of wind-swept cliffs and buried beneath huge overlying expanses of unbroken blanket peat, is a great maze of dry-stone walls. Radiocarbon dating of the peats beneath the walls revealed they were built almost 5,000 years ago, during the Neolithic period. Pollen analytical studies of the

peats lent weight to the archaeological evidence that the large fields enclosed by the walls had been used to stockade cattle rather than to protect crops. This ancient field system, in a place unsuited to modern cattle farming, is the most extensive and best preserved in Europe.

The techniques used to build the walls at Ceide are still used throughout Ireland today, but wall building in the uplands was at its height almost 5,000 years later, during the nineteenth century when marginal land was brought under cultivation to support the growing population. Those newly-created, small and unproductive fields are no longer tilled but are still easy to recognise high above the present limit of farming. Their surfaces are ridged with abandoned lazy beds once used to grow potatoes and each field may still be edged by stone

Hedges of whin in flower along an upland roadside.

Gappy hedges and gappy walls

The technique of laying hedges by cutting, bending and weaving branches to form a stock-proof barrier is infrequently practiced in Ireland. This gappy hedge, cut by machine and reinforced by barbed wire is typical of lowland areas (top).

The stone walls of uplands and rocky areas are both boundaries and shelter for livestock. In some areas they are also a way of disposing of the huge number of stones cleared from land to make pasture or crop fields.

walls in decent repair. Many upland walls only partly enclosed the unworked, rush-infested fields and ultimately these walls dwindle and vanish into the open higher land. These half-marked places may be the outer fringes and last remnants of other prehistoric systems of enclosure. The walls have been absorbed into the landscape's later record of a time when thousands of people left the barren uplands after the Great Potato Famine of the 1840s. The pre-famine walls are less important now as boundaries but still provide life-saving shelter from the winter winds for the hardy mountain sheep which have taken the place of the small prehistoric cattle.

Whether ancient or modern, the waist to breast-high walls are strongly made of local stones, set skilfully one upon another without the use of mortar. The stability of the wall depends on the unsealed gaps through which the wind passes. The earth-packed double wall or stone hedge of lowland Cornwall is a very solid structure when compared with the lacework walls of the Burren, Connemara or almost any other Irish upland. Numerous species of lichen or mosses adapted to withstand extremes of aridity may thrive, but flowering plants on these walls are few as the gaps rarely accumulate enough organic material where plants may root. The luxuriant growths of grass or clover are only at the sheltered base of the wall.

Walls are not restricted to the uplands and in the lowlands many of the oldest and botanically most interesting are not round fields but surround old estates and gardens. Some of these large walls support luxuriant plant growth on their sides and tops with some species found almost in no other places. Other plants, which grow better in more favoured places, can colonise the accumulated soil in the crevices. There are walls in County Tipperary on which grow large plants of navelwort (*Umbilicus rupestris*). The succulent navelwort roots in the small crevices between the stones and is tolerant of an erratic water supply. The succulent species of stonecrops (*Sedum* species) are as well adapted to life in natural rock crevices as to flourishing in crannies on well-lit walls. The nature of

The cracks in this ancient castle wall provide a home for the wallflower, red valerian and the fine, trailing ivy-leaved toadflax.

In many upland areas, the tiny stone-walled fields have long been abandoned. Here, the fields are still cut for hay in summer and grazed in the winter.

Pellitory-of-the-wall also thrives on the lime-rich mortar of old stone walls. Here it is growing on an abbey wall as it did probably in medieval times when it was valued for its medicinal properties.

Ivy-leaved toadflax is delicate in appearance but copes with the harsh dry conditions of a stone wall.

the rock from which the wall is built may influence the plants which grow on it, for example, some stonecrops have need for limestone while others prefer granite.

Some plants are so associated with walls that this is reflected in their common or Latin names. A fine example is Pellitory-of-the-wall (*Parietaria judaica*). A plant enthusiast and rail traveller, coming to Dublin from the north, may meet the plant growing at the base of the wall outside Connolly Railway Station. Wall barley (*Hordeum murinum*) is found growing on walls in the southern counties where it is equally at home in the cracks in the pavement. The preference for walls of the very common,

but introduced, ivy-leaved toadflax (*Cymbalaria muralis*) is apparent in the second part of its botanical name as *muralis* is used of plants associated with walls. The plant is common, protruding from walls in towns and country where its small purple and yellow flowers resemble those of the garden snapdragon (*Antirrhinum*) to which it is distantly related. Another wall-loving garden escape, in the same plant family (Scrophulariaceae) as the ivy-leaved toadflax, is the fairy foxglove (*Erinus alpinus*) with its dainty pink flowers which in early summer brighten the high forbidding walls of the old county gaol in Downpatrick in County Down.

The fairy foxglove growing on the old gaol wall in Downpatrick, County Down.

The bright carmine flowers of the red valerian (*Centranthus ruber*) also crown the tops of old walls.

Many plants will tolerate life on the sides of a wall even though they may do better in more favoured places. Herb Robert will grow and flower on walls which provide it with a meagre living. Its stunted and starved, stiff, little stems and leaves may remain throughout the spring and summer, reddish with autumnal tints, while the same plant growing in damper and better fed conditions becomes large, green, lank and floppy. The bittersweet (*Solanum dulcamara*), although a plant of woodland edge and hedges, seems to be getting commoner on the walls of old houses in towns while the increase in buddleja in similar places receives attention in Chapter 8.

Whereas much is known about the time when the first walls were built, less is known about the history of hedges in Ireland, although there are records in the mid-seventeenth century Civil Survey

Many of the native lime-loving ferns such as this rustyback fern now thrive in the lime-rich mortar of old walls. Here it grows with herb Robert.

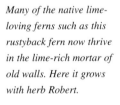

commenting on 'quicksett' hedges in County Tipperary. The hedge is the commonest means of landscape division in the lowlands with their long and complex history of mixed agriculture. Careful management is needed for keeping animals from ruining crops and permanent or temporary barriers are needed to help stock control. In the early medieval Irish 'Brehon Laws', enclosures and barriers based on permanent and temporary ditches and moveable panels of wattle were described. The pattern of some well-established medieval fields in the Irish midlands indicates permanence before the eighteenth century, when there is an increase in descriptions in the historical record of hedges or temporary barriers which acted like hedges. It is beyond the scope of this book to trace the spread of hedged enclosure in the late seventeenth and eighteenth centuries but the following details serve to emphasise how patchy was the expansion of hedging in those days.

Maps, surveys and descriptions of Ulster in the seventeenth century rarely indicate enclosure. The Raven Maps of the Clandeboye Estate, compiled in 1625, only separate bog from pasture. Writing of an adjacent area 100 years later, Walter Harris makes some mention of enclosure but it was of a very temporary nature. He says of the Copeland Islands

they have no fences in the islands; but to preserve their corn from trespass they fold their cattle within enclosures raised of sods and let them out to graze at the proper season and watch and hurd (sic) them as it is called there; and the same custom is used in the Barony of Ardes and most other parts of this county.

Hawthorn, quickthorn or May blossom. This is the plant of the 'quicksett' hedges mentioned in mid-seventeenth-century texts.

Hawthorn flowers are like those of its relative the apple.

The mass of red hawthorn berries provide winter food for birds.

Hillsborough as '*a pretty English like enclosed countrey (*sic*)*'. The hedges of lowland Ireland today are thus the most recent addition to a landscape which has undergone extensive and drastic remodelling over the last 5,000 years.

What then is a hedge? It is a boundary made of trees and shrubs planted in a line and separating one field from another or from lanes and roads. In many counties, the hedge will be of hawthorn or quickthorn, possibly blackthorn (*Prunus spinosa*), including occasional trees such as ash, elm, beech, sycamore or oak. Thorny brambles and

This account contrasts with one written by Dr Molyneaux in 1708 who describes the area around Lisburn and

wild roses as well as various wild flowers are at its base. The modern hedge may also include large clumps of dead whins or furze, possibly even an old bed frame, all pushed into the many gaps at the bottom of the hedge and through it strands of rusty barbed wire nailed to rickety and irregularly-placed fence posts. Access to the fields beyond is through a gate which may be properly hinged on a gate post or otherwise secured with assorted wire and twine. The hedge management techniques such as 'laying', which makes the impenetrable hedge the pride of the English lowland farmer, are confined to a few counties in Ireland. Although, on close inspection, the collection of materials which make up an Irish hedge are less than lovely, the hedge works well enough even if a bit gappy at the base.

The hedge is rarely planted directly into the fields which it separates but rather planted on a raised earth bank, often with a drainage channel at its base. In some parts of the country the raised part is called a bank with the drainage channel known as the ditch, but in other areas the bank is called the ditch and the drainage channel or ditch is termed the sheugh! A visitor who does not know the local meaning of 'ditch' can become mightily confused.

Woody hedge plants
In Ireland, as throughout much of Great Britain, the commonest hedging shrub is

This piece of feckless 'hedge trimming' by a county council typifies what still passes for hedge maintenance in many areas.

the hawthorn. This woody member of the rose family is ideally suited to forming secure, stock-proof barriers as it grows rapidly on a wide range of soils, is oblivious to hardship, and a hedge grown from it is relatively easy to maintain. In Ireland, hawthorns are managed by cutting and the shape of the hedge can be maintained by an annual pruning with tools which now include a mechanised hedge cutter capable of slashing hundreds of metres of sides and hedge tops in a few days. After cutting by this method, a hedge can look a sorry sight with the branches as often broken as cut but it is not all calamity as the

This six-legged fairy thorn is clipped each year to maintain its unusual shape.

hardy hawthorn recovers rapidly and is reinvigorated with huge numbers of vivid-green leaves and a great wealth of flower and fruit in ensuing years.

The hawthorn hedge in full spring flower is one of the glories of the Irish countryside when, in May, the hundreds of thousands of twiggy hawthorn bushes rapidly transform under a foam of white blossom, often flushed with pink. On a calm day, the sickly-sweet perfume of the flowers is overpowering and this may

This single hawtorn bush is all that remains of a thorn hedge, but is still trimmed each year to maintain its flat top. Note the earth bank on which the original thorn hedge was planted.

have some part in the old custom of never bringing flowering hawthorn into the home. Some say it is a witch's flower while others say that the hawthorn is linked to Christ's Crown of Thorns.

In autumn the ripening berries or haws provide nourishing food for many species of birds and mammals, including foxes, who find the fruit palatable, but to most people the berries are dry and insipid.

Solitary hawthorn trees growing in the centre of fields must be the safest plants in Ireland. Nobody interferes with the 'fairy thorns', as these lonely trees are called. The power of the fairy thorn tree to cause harm to anyone who abuses it is recorded all over Ireland. It is said that the hand of the one who hurts the thorn tree is in turn maimed while others have died under mysterious circumstances after cutting or uprooting a fairy thorn tree. Many trees are

carefully tended as the old ways still command respect in Ireland in the town as well as the country, even in this cynical age.

In many hedges, the hawthorn is the commonest representative of the rose family but there are many others, for example, the blackthorn, blackberry, wild cherry, wild rose, wild plum,

Damson hedges were planted both for their crop and as a field boundary in County Armagh.

Blackthorn in flower.

The brilliant white flowers of the wild cherry (*Prunus avium*) are a feature of many hedges and the white flowers, backed by the bronze of the emerging leaves, are visible for some distance. Occasional wild apple trees (*Malus sylvestris*) are seen in Irish hedges. In flower, the apple blossom in the hedge looks like any in an orchard but in autumn the hedge apple's small fruit may point to the tree's obscure origins. Some may be true native apples while others are possibly the progeny of native crab apples crossed with cultivated fruit. Some may even have been grown from the seeds in a discarded apple core.

Two smaller members of the rose family are common in hedges throughout the country, the wild rose (*Rosa canina*) and the blackberry or bramble. Both are famously thorny and both are equally well known either for the beauty of their flowers or the excellence of their fruit. The wild or dog rose has beautiful white to rich pink flowers, each with a contrasting ring of golden stamens in the centre. Parts of Leitrim are called Wild Rose Country and rightly so as the hedges there are garlanded with the simple, single flowers which contrast with the many-petalled flowers of the garden rose. Small double roses are, however, seen from time to time in hedges throughout the country and it is debatable if these are variants of true wild roses or ones which have acquired some cultivated rose genes. There are a few hedges in Leitrim where small, pale

damson, and apple. The blackthorn is almost as common as the hawthorn in some hedges but is rarely planted deliberately as its suckering habit lets it freely colonise the hedge. The first spring flush of hedgerow petals are often those of the blackthorn whose small, dingy white flowers may open in March when frosts are still common.

The blackthorn is in the same genus (*Prunus*) as the plum. Wild plum trees can grow to considerable size in sheltered spots, while their cousins, the damsons, are less often seen. The damson hedges around Loughgall in County Armagh are distinguishable from the blackthorn which is in flower at the same time. Later in the year, the damson's purple fruit will not be confused with the blue-bloomed sloe.

The variability in both flower shape and in fruit of blackberry arises from its genetics.

The Irish dog rose, found near Holywood, County Down and described by Templeton.

pink, double-flowered roses grow and these would be well worthy of garden cultivation. Ireland has a special rose which was found in 1795 near Holywood, County Down by Templeton, the famous Irish botanist. The rose, known as the Irish rose (*Rosa* x *hibernica*), is a hybrid between the wild dog rose and the burnet rose (*R. pimpinellifolia*). Although no longer in the wild where Templeton found it, it is now a cherished garden plant.

The fruit of the rose, the hip, is produced in autumn and is scarlet and shiny with numerous fluffy seeds within, but is not the simple fruit it appears to be. Like many of that family, the showy, brightly-coloured structure, apparently a fruit is, in fact, the swollen top of the

The yellowish-green flowers of alexanders, an introduced member of the carrot family, are now common on east-coast road sides.

The native cow parsley is also a common hedge-base plant, flowering in early summer.

flower stem with the true fruits concealed within. Many plants in the rose family are the ancestors of popular 'fruits' such as the apple, pear and strawberry, all of which produce complex stuctures called 'false fruits'. The false fruit is a highly adapted flower stem which becomes coloured, juicy and sweet after the flower has been fertilized and ultimately surrounds the true fruit, as with the apple, or it may carry large numbers of true fruit on its surface, as does the strawberry.

The blackberry or bramble is recognised throughout Ireland as the tastiest of the fruits of the hedge and each autumn scores of families set off along country lanes to collect blackberries for pies, jams and jellies. Most people have their favourite picking places and know where the best berries are to be found as in some places the fruit is plump and juicy while in others the berries are small, dry and full of seeds. This variation in fruit quality is not only the result of soil, aspect and the weather in the preceding summer but also closely linked to the genetics of the blackberry. For this reason many botanical texts will not give the plant's botanical name solely as *Rubus fruticosus* but as *Rubus fruticosus* sens.

lat., the appendage sens. lat. (*sensu lato*) meaning 'in the wide sense' and referring to the wide variation within the species. Work on mapping the numerous forms within the species is ongoing and much has been detailed about the plant's bewilderingly wide range of growth form and flowering habit.

Most of the shrubs growing in an Irish hedge complete their annual flowering in the spring but it is not until June that the blackberry is in full flower. Like its close relatives, the wild roses, the bloom of the blackberry is made up of small, pale pink petals surrounding a ring of stamens which in turn surround the female parts of the flower. It is these which, when fertilised, will produce the familiar fruit.

Look closely at the blackberry flowers in a stretch of hedge and you may see that some are pinker than others. The palest pink petal may be mottled or striped with darker pink, giving the flower the look of a tiny blob of raspberry-ripple ice cream. The flowers also vary in size and in some places, especially in County Wicklow, there are flowering blackberries whose striking blossoms would be worthy of garden cultivation.

The showy flowers and fruits of the hedge are not the only woody species which grow there for most also include trees which have been spared cutting back. Big ash trees are common in hedges throughout the country but oak, elm, willows of various sorts, hazel and poplars with lesser shrubs like elder, holly, the pink-fruited spindle and scarlet-berried guelder-rose are also common in some districts. The big hedgerow trees may also include the non-native beech and sycamore joined by smaller *Laburnum* or lilac (*Syringa*). The fuchsia hedges of the west of Ireland are well known and are described in Chapter 8, but the *Laburnum* hedges in County Armagh have only recently been described. Short lengths of lilac hedge, seen in some midland counties, have probably resulted from colonisation by the suckers of a few introduced plants.

In many southern counties the high hedges fringing many roads are almost exclusively of well-grown ash or beech trees and these stately trees give the countryside a prosperous air. Many of these hedges are on the edge of well managed farms where good timber has

This line of beech trees was once the boundary hedge of a big estate. With time the hedge has dwindled leaving the beech trees in a line across the fields.

Elder in blossom.

been planted over the years. The lovely, high hedges of Wicklow contain frequent oaks, giving welcome shade on a hot summer day.

The hedge as a source of timber was a valuable addition to the agricultural economy in former times as, since the final demise of extensive woodland, Ireland has been short of timber. When hedges were first extensively planted

Modern farm machinery demands much larger field units. The line of an old hedge can still be seen in the foreground.

Many of the plants of this hedge base, such as the ferns and bluebell, are woodland species.

Oak and elm, ash and sycamore were used throughout the farm and the lesser species like willow or poplar would not have been despised. Every twig and scrap had a use, including kindling for the turf fire as turf is a difficult fuel to set alight. The elder or boortree may have been less useful than most as its hollow wood has little strength but when dry even this can be used to get the fire perked up. Estimations of the age of a hedge, based on the number of woody species it contains are not applicable in Ireland. A combination of factors such as more than one type of tree being used, the inclusion of hedgerow timber and the thinning of an unmanaged hedge due to age make any mathematical formula based on woody species likely to be unworkable.

during the eighteenth century, farmers were expected to include ash, oak and elm in the new hedges, with legislation in place to ensure that these useful species were planted. Whether or not farmers took much heed of the legislation is a matter for debate but with it or without it, the trees now familiar in every hedgerow were planted and their timber valued for all manner of uses. For example, ash wood is straight and smooth, making good tool handles as it rarely splinters and when cut back it will rapidly produce young growth which can be left to develop into thicknesses suitable for use around the farm. To this day, a young ash branch, complete with leaves, will be cut and carried by the farmer as an aid when herding cattle or sheep.

Hedges today

The expansion of hedged enclosure in the eighteenth and early nineteenth centuries was one aspect of the agricultural reforms which had impact throughout Ireland and Great Britain. The sizes of fields surrounded by the new hedges were determined in part by earlier practice. New means of tillage, crop rotation and improved field drainage, coupled with demands of the new and improved agricultural machines such as ploughs, which were coming into the country at that time, all affected the development of the hedged landscape.

In the last two decades of the twentieth century, miles of hedges were removed although this was never on the huge scale seen in the arable lands of southern England. With the removal of the hedges came strong opposition from individuals and conservation bodies who saw grave risk to wildlife whose only home was the hedge. There has been a revision of thinking on the wisdom of hedge removal and now farmers are encouraged to maintain and even replant hedging. One of the powerful arguments used in defence of the hedge stated that it was a form of woodland as it supported many species of woodland plants and animals. This analogy should not, however, be carried too far as a hedge is far from a wood as a provider of complex interdependent environments. For example, the many trees in a woodland offer mutual protection from extremes of climate, in contrast to a hedge where at least one side is constantly exposed to wind and weather. Hedges probably resemble some ancient woodland edges where the light-demanding tree species and their attendant wild flowers could thrive. The flora of the banks on which the hedge shrubs are planted is worth examining. The shady banks are home to yellow-flowered wood avens (*Geum urbanum*), another member of the rose family in which the hedges are so rich. The banks of the Kerry lanes glow lime-green in spring with the Irish spurge (*Euphorbia hyberna*). Commoner hedgerow plants are the pungent-leaved hedge woundwort (*Stachys sylvatica*), wild strawberry (*Fragaria vesca*) and the white-flowered greater stitchwort (*Stellaria holostea*).

There are, throughout the country, hedges which almost defy botanical

Wood avens, the small-flowered relative of the water avens (Chapter 5), is often seen in Irish hedges.

colonised by this most opportunistic of grasses. Entirely satisfactory hedges comprising dense hazel with elm or beech through which grow honeysuckle and ivy with reeds and pendulous sedge (*Carex pendula*) growing high as a man are not recorded in the standard texts.

At the foot of many hedges there is a shallow channel known variously as the ditch or sheugh. Wet throughout the year with water drained from field and lane surface, they offer a home to some plants more suited to the lake shores than the edge of a road. On Clare Island off the Mayo coast, what sparse hedges there are have water-loving plants growing at their feet and these include the blue-flowered brooklime (*Veronica beccabunga*). Marsh cinquefoil and fragrant water mint are seen in ditches in the midlands along with bur-marigold (*Bidens tripartita*) and even water-cress (*Nasturtium officinale*) with its need for permanent moisture.

Two unconventional hedge plants. Above: the common reed forms a hedge along a lowland roadside and below: the New Zealand flax forms an effective barrier round this coastal pasture.

description because they contain such peculiar mixes of species. For example, the reed has none of the qualities associated with the plants good for making a hedge but in some western counties damp hedges have been heavily

In this chapter much has been made of the hedge at its liveliest, filled with sprouting new leaves and flowers or red and purple with autumn berries. It would be negligent if the hedge in winter was ignored. By the end of November most of the leaves have gone, the ash tree is hung with bunches of seeds looking just like keys and the last of the blackberries droop mummified on the twigs, providing food for birds when the weather starts to turn nasty. But walk out on the morning of the winter solstice, 21 December, and look

at the outline of the hedge against the sky as the sun rises.

The hedge may be squat from years of cutting back, crowning the tops of drumlins or taller in the fertile fields of the midlands and showing the bird nests no longer hidden by the leaves of summer. As the solstice sky changes from rose to gold, the hedge gives definition to the fields now denuded of summer's crops. The trees mark the sky with black trunks and finer branches.

The sleeping hedge makes a black filigree against the lightening sky but still does its job by giving shelter to cattle and sheep with their earliest lambs. In January days the hedge drips with rain, is iced with frost or bends beneath snow but soon the hedge begins to turn yellow with the catkins of willow and then of hazel and so the cycle of life held in an Irish hedge begins again.

The red valerian is seen on the tops of old walls in some areas, particularly near the sea.

8 WEEDS AND ALIENS

The plants which are the focus of this chapter do not comprise a clearly defined system of vegetation such as a woodland or bog. To a varying extent, the places where these plants grow are the product of a host of human activities. Our attitudes to weeds and alien plants are as fickle as human nature. It is in places as contrasting as the newly-exposed soils of a motorway embankment, old cultivated fields and commercial forestry plots that weeds may thrive. Aliens, plants from other countries that are making a new home in Ireland, have often escaped from gardens. That both weeds and aliens are fit only for eradication by chemicals or the hoe would be the view of some people, while others enjoy the beautiful colours of some 'wild' flowers once grouped amongst the most pernicious of weeds and the lovely blossoms of some of the most aggressively-invasive aliens.

What is a weed?

Even to lump the plants which we call weeds and aliens under one heading is a reflection of our attitudes to them. Most

Common weeds in a vegetable garden. Their rapid germination and fast growth rate allow them to out-compete the cultivated plants.

Self-sown weeds adorn the sides of a newly-constructed motorway slip-road in Belfast city centre.

Dandelion, daisy and
speedwell are common
lawn weeds, flowering here
in grass which has not
been cut.

*Hairy bitter-cress in midwinter. The ripe
seedpods show that frost does not deter this
hardy weed from setting seed.*

*Stinging nettle flowering in
midsummer.*

weeds such as dandelions, nettles and
docks are not introduced from other
lands but are native plants. Only a few
introduced species like the
rhododendron have become such

invasive aliens that they too are classed
as weeds. Neither are all native weeds
and introduced aliens universally
despised nor considered undesirable.
The cornflower (*Centaurea cyanus*),
once a common weed in the flax fields
of the north of Ireland, is now a very
rare and protected wild flower growing
only where old ways of tillage still
survive. The rhododendron, which
comes from central and southern Europe
and is regarded as a pest in the southern
native oakwoods of Ireland, now
features on postcards as a part of a
colourful natural landscape, with never a
mention of its origins. It is we humans
who make weeds of the plants once
restricted to a narrow range of habitats
and, but for our actions, there would be
no alien species joining our native flora.

Weeds and aliens are not easily
separated as they have characteristics in
common, but in general terms weeds are
native plants which grow where they are
not wanted – in gardens, farmland and
forestry. Alien plants are first introduced
to environments strongly influenced by

This artificial hill of topsoil is covered by docks. The soil was moved as part of development work for an industrial site near Downpatrick in County Down. The same project dug out lake muds formed at the end of the last glaciation, including the skull and antler of the extinct Giant Irish deer. From pollen analysis we know that docks like these covered the loose soils as the last glaciation ended.

people but can then invade natural or semi-natural vegetation without further human help. Weeds are unloved by gardeners and farmers because they compete with crops for light, water and nutrients or 'make the place look untidy'. Additionally, some weeds wage chemical warfare on the crops with which they grow by producing, from their roots, toxins which may damage the crop. Aliens may pose a threat to already vulnerable native species as they may alter an environment to the detriment of its original inhabitants.

Garden weeds

The commonest weeds such as the stinging nettle (*Urtica dioica*), dock (*Rumex species*), daisy (*Bellis perennis*) and dandelion (*Taraxacum group*) are readily recognisable and will grow vigorously where humans have been. If one may ask 'what were hedgehogs

called before there were hedges' then we can also ask 'where did weeds grow before there was agriculture'? Most native weeds are amongst our oldest native plants, having been in Ireland since the end of the last glaciation 15,000 years ago, 7,000 years before the first cattle or primitive wheat were brought here by Neolithic people.

The successful weeds of today must be able to cope with the disturbed soils and extremes of climate, conditions like those after the last of the great glaciers had gone from Ireland more than 15,000 years ago. The newly-exposed soils of the glacial ridges and moraines were very different from those of today, being unstable and having little humus but with abundant nutrients. The fossil record shows that these raw soils were rapidly smothered by docks and mugwort which could establish and produce seed where little else would survive. By showing their

Dandelions make a brief blaze of yellow along many Irish roadsides in late April.

The dandelion's flowering season is brief and soon the roadside ribbons of yellow are replaced by the silver of seed heads.

capacity for being able to live under duress, these plants have the properties we think of as characterising weeds. These same plants later became weeds because humans re-create, through land management and cultivation, the shifting soils similar to those found at the edge of melting ice sheets.

The origin of these ancient cold-tolerant plants is unclear. They may have followed the retreat of the ice and returned to Ireland from a more distant place, or they may have remained throughout the cold of the last glacial maximum in small populations in favoured places in the area now close to the southern Irish coast. The weight of fossil evidence does not tip the balance of probability in either direction.

Whatever the means of their expansion, they soon took advantage of improving conditions and in doing so began the process of returning decomposed plant material to the raw soil.

What are the properties of a successful weed? Amongst others, they must be able, by germinating rapidly or growing swiftly, to thrive under conditions which would stifle or kill other plants. The speed at which some can grow and set seed is almost breath-taking. Some can germinate, grow, set seed and die within a few weeks, while others have a range of longer-term strategies. Hairy bitter-cress (*Cardamine hirsuta*) can germinate and thrive in suburban gardens even during an Irish winter and can complete a number of generations in only one growing season. Others like the annual chickweed (*Stellaria media*) not only produce copious seed each year but can spread if a small, broken bit of the leafy stem with attached roots can make contact with the soil. Any gardener growing peas will grumble about the apparently magical ease with which tiny scraps of chickweed can re-root even after careful hand-weeding, especially when the weather is warm and moist.

Others weeds such as dock or nettle have a different strategy to thwart the rigorous gardener. The dock or docken, as it is often called in Ireland by those searching for its leaves after suffering recent nettle stings, is as fine a native weed as could be desired. Docks are great opportunists; being perennial, they can survive harsh conditions, even when all their leaves have gone, because of starchy food stored in their long roots. Dock leaves may be wrenched off by the

gardener, shrivelled by chemical weed killers or wither and die in winter but they will grow again from the root stock the following year, and are joined by young plants newly-germinated from the large numbers of seeds produced on the plant's tall, rusty-coloured tops. Dock seeds have the ability to germinate and grow vigorously in the crevices and crannies of shallow soil where other plants would not survive.

The nettle, whose sting the dock leaf soothes, is a native plant which, in contrast to the dock, grows well where human and animal waste has enriched the soil with nitrogenous nutrients. Archaeologists recognise that nettles grow on ancient dung heaps and gardeners know that a good bed of nettles is a sure sign of fertile soil beneath.

Similar survival techniques to those used by docks are employed by the

Successful annual garden weeds germinate faster than vegetable seeds and grow more vigorously than the crop. These are characteristics that served the plant well in the disturbed soils and harsh conditions of a frozen world.

Coltsfoot flowers in early spring either just before the leaves expand or, as here, just as the leaves are emerging.

The seed heads of coltsfoot are similar to, but smaller than, those of dandelion.

small flowers. After the yellow flower-parts have faded they are replaced by the fluffy 'clocks' known to every child. The 'clocks' are the plant's seed heads and each seed can drift off in the slightest breeze soon to take root and grow another dandelion plant.

Those familiar seed heads are the product of the dandelion's advanced reproductive system. Dandelions belong to the daisy family which contains some of the most advanced flowering plants. A dandelion flower may be capable of producing seed without pollination, allowing each flower to independently generate a further crop of fly-away seeds to strengthen the local population or expand into other areas. This ability to reproduce without pollination is met with in the cold climates of Arctic and Alpine areas and may be seen as a relic of the ancient physiology of the plant which adapted it so well to post-glacial conditions.

Related to the dandelion is the coltsfoot. The flowers are one of the first to appear in spring in Ireland and are usually produced before the leaves. Coltsfoot is becoming a common city weed and is able to push up through cracks in concrete and tarmac. It is also a plant of sand dunes and is common along road sides.

Some of our most common weeds may have been relatively rare in ancient times, but flourished with the start of agriculture. The ancient pollen record shows the first of these weeds to be the

dandelion. As well as having a long tap root which stores food, dandelions can make great quantities of easily dispersed seeds. Its flowers are one of the glories of the spring countryside, making a sunny-yellow border to the hedges through millions of wide-open flowers. Each 'flower' is in fact a cluster of many

ribwort plantain (*Plantago lanceolata*) which spread in Ireland with the arrival of agriculture and marked the start of the Neolithic period, almost 6,000 years ago. Plantain is a native plant that may well have been growing here since the retreat of the ice, but there is a dramatic increase in the amount of its pollen at the same time as the appearance of the first cereal pollen grains in the ancient record. Both types of pollen will have blown onto the bog surface from the nearby fields of the first farmers.

It is not known if the increase in plantains occurred because the native plantain exploited the newly-turned soil or if plantains grew from seeds contaminating primitive wheat seed brought to Ireland by the first farmers. In all probability, both circumstances happened simultaneously and show just how difficult it is to separate the true native plants from imported strains of the same species.

Plantain leaf-shape changes according to the surroundings of the plant. In short grass the plant has a rosette of leaves growing almost flush with the surface of the soil where it can withstand trampling, whether from the feet of the small cattle raised in Ireland 5,000 years ago or, today, the feet of footballers and hikers.

The ribwort plantain in long grass (above) and in short grass, grazed by rabbits (below). Plants with this ability to adapt to different growing conditions are termed 'plastic'.

Cornflower. This picture is of plants grown in a garden because the cornflower is now rare in the wild in Ireland.

In long grass the leaves are especially long and slender, with a tendency to grow upright. Ribwort plantain shares with the dock and the dandelion a long taproot from which new shoots arise if the head of the plant is cut off.

Farmland weeds

The weeds whose distinctive pollen is seen at the start of the agricultural pollen record are native species which have successfully adapted to change as our landscape was moulded by climate and people. There are, however, other weeds such as the pretty blue cornflower which may not be native but probably came in with new crops in prehistoric or early historic times. Nevertheless, these naturalised plants have been part of our landscape for so long that they are as much a part of our botanical heritage as wheat and barley.

The history of farmland weeds in

Ireland is poorly understood since the fossilized seed record is fragmentary and the pollen record gives little insight into the origins of these insect-pollinated species which produce only small amounts of pollen. Records from medieval documents make comments on weeds amongst corn but confirmation of the precise species is never possible. In Great Britain, the history of some weed species such as the cornflower or the pinkish-purple corn cockle (*Agrostemma githago*) is better understood; it is possible that corn cockle arrived in Britain with the Romans. Less showy is the grass darnel (*Lolium temulentum*) which may be the 'barren wheat' mentioned in the Bible. It was a great trouble to farmers years ago as darnel-infested grain produced poisonous flour which could lead to blindness and ultimately death. Corn cockle seed ground in bread flour made the loaf unwholesome as it also contained poisonous chemicals. The stems of cornflowers are so tough that they are said to have blunted the reaper's sickle.

It is worth noting that some early cereal-harvesting techniques will favour the dispersal of tall weeds. In the past, cereals were not reaped at ground level but cut about 60cm above the ground. The farmer grasped a handful of the crop and its weeds just below the crop's seed head. The entire handful was then sliced off by the blade of the sickle. Weeds like mugwort, poppy (*Papaver* species), cornflower and corn cockle are

Common cornfield weeds of the past still spring up in patches which chemical sprays have missed. Here corn marigold and fumitory brighten this wheat field.

Corn marigold on a wheat field margin.

all much the same height as barley and oats and had their seedheads collected with the ripe grain.

As today's seed for the following year's sowing is efficiently cleaned of impurities like weed seeds, in the second half of the twentieth century, the virtual extermination of darnel and cornflower from Ireland's fields has been swift and successful. Darnel and cornflowers are now restricted to a few fields in County Limerick and the Aran Islands where locally-saved cereal seed, especially rye, and older farming practices, conserve these rarities. This is in strong contrast to the fields of less than 100 years ago when the great Irish botanist Robert Lloyd Praeger commented in 1901 that darnel was common throughout Ireland. Cornflower may never have been as widely distributed as darnel, growing

more abundantly in the flax fields of the north and east of Ireland where this crop was commonly grown until the Second World War. Because its seeds do not survive for long periods in the soil, corn cockle is now very uncommon.

Not all of the weeds of arable crops have disappeared, with some like the common poppy (*Papaver rhoeas*) and the corn marigold (*Chrysanthemum segetum*) still locally common throughout Ireland. Seeds of the corn marigold and corn cockle were found in archaeological excavations of a site in

Rosebay willow herb or fireweed has increased in recent decades in Ireland. Here it colonises a recently felled conifer plantation.

Dublin occupied 1,000 years ago, showing that the weed was growing here in those times. The corn marigold continues to hold its own and can be seen with other field weeds among the modern awned wheats now commonly grown throughout Ireland.

The common poppy is an annual and does well where land is opened by the plough. In the 1950s, they were common along the edges of fields of oats in north County Down where one author remembers the cheerful red flowers just visible over a stone wall beside a field of oats near the village of Groomsport. Poppies still grow in that area, especially on the grassy edges of the paths leading down to the nearby beach but the oat field is now part of the garden of a modern home. If that garden was dug up again it is likely that poppies would grow anew as poppy seed may remain viable for up to 80 years.

It is questionable if poppies were as common in Ireland in the past as they remain today in southern England, where the banks of the motorways and the fields in Devon are splashed with patches of red. North of Birmingham there seem to be fewer poppies and nowhere in Ireland can anything like the poppy-flanked English motorway be seen. In Ireland, poppies are common enough, but in small groups, never as great red sheets.

Under EU directives to control agricultural over-production, some fields are now being left fallow for a year between crops. This is providing a new opportunity for some arable weeds as the

A 'clean' wheat field where crop spraying has eliminated all the traditional cornfield weeds.

illustration of the field of knotgrass (*Polygonum specie*s) shows.

Weeds are not normally a problem in pasture because grazing keeps them under control. Many are even more nutritious than grasses, but one pasture invader, the ragwort (*Senecio jacobaea*), classed as a noxious weed, is poisonous

A field in County Tipperary left fallow after the harvesting of barley is home to a range of fast-growing weeds, including two species of the pink-flowered knotgrass.

Seeds of traditional cornfield weeds and pasture weeds are now available for gardeners to re-create the weedy fields of their grandfathers. Use of wild flower seed mixtures imported from outside Ireland may build up problems for the future as they will have a different genetic make-up from native stock and may replace or dilute the native population. This is of particular concern where the native population is very small.

Oxford ragwort is now at home in the city streets of Dublin and Belfast.

to cattle. Normally cattle will not eat the plant in the field, but will eat hay containing it. The toxins may also be present in honey if the plants are visited by bees. The ragwort is increasing in Ireland and is a common plant of waste ground along with the rosebay willow-herb or fireweed (*Chamaenerion angustifolium*). The latter has increased dramatically during the twentieth century and is now the main coloniser of recently-felled forestry plantations.

What would a nineteenth-century farmer have made of the packets of wild-flower seed for sale in any garden centre in spring? The conservation-minded gardener can buy seeds of poppy, cornflower and corn cockle, the very weeds which our farming ancestors would have been pleased to be rid off. To many, it is a joy to see these brightly coloured flowers again, the seed having been yet again imported from places where the plants still thrive. The story comes full circle with cornflower and corn cockle seeds being brought into Ireland, but this time knowingly and for the delight of the gardener, not the bane of the farmer.

Indian balsam growing along the River Lagan near Belfast where it has spread extensively. The explosive seedpods contribute to its rapid spread.

The fuchsia, from Chile, seems well adapted to the Irish climate. It is used as the motif for jewellery and pottery sold in numerous Irish art and craft shops.

Montbretia is now a common sight on roadsides.

Alien plants

We have seen that our weeds may be plain or pretty but what of the alien species, some of which are now common throughout the country? We know a little more of the history of these newcomers to our modern flora, as almost all have been introduced during the later historic period, for which there is a better written record. For example,

the Oxford ragwort (*Senecio squalidus*), a native of central and southern Europe, was first seen on walls in Oxford in 1794. By the 1980s it was frequent in southern Ireland and is now a common weed of city streets and waste ground throughout the country. Fifty years ago the various shades of pink of the flowers of the Indian balsam (*Impatiens glandulifera*) were not to be seen along many Irish river banks. During the 1950s its spread in the north of Ireland was monitored by the botanists at the Ulster Museum in Belfast, who enlisted the help of local plant enthusiasts in plotting its distribution at that time. Today it is widespread close to water courses.

Alien plants are bewildering in their behaviour. Large numbers of non-native species have been introduced to Ireland as plants for the garden. The majority 'know their place' and stay within the bounds of horticulture but there are some that leave the garden and find new homes in the semi-wild places where most do little if any harm. The bright orange-flowered montbretia (*Tritonia crocosmiflora*; also known as *Crocosmia crocosmiflora*) can be found throughout the country, growing amongst lank grass and admired by many as a pleasant addition to hedgerows and rough banks. It is a harmless perennial which grows from an underground corm and seems well-suited to life in Ireland although it is of South African origin, via some horticultural hybridising.

The fuchsia (*Fuchsia magellanica*) originates from Chile but is now virtually adopted as a beautiful and harmless Irish native. The fuchsia hedges of the western and north-eastern coasts are glorious when in flower and in a good year the foliage is almost invisible beneath the elegant purple and red flowers. Fuchsia rarely sets viable seed in Ireland and, like the rhododendron, it is featured on postcards showing the beauties of the Irish countryside.

The buddleja (*Buddleja davidii*) is another alien that adds colour to wild and waste places in Ireland. It grows well in the dry conditions of building

Buddleja or butterfly bush rapidly colonises dry waste ground.

The beauty of rhododendron belies its aggressive nature.

Rhododendron spreading vigorously on thin blanket peat in the Mourne Mountains.

sites and motorway banks and is often seen growing on the chimney stacks of old buildings in city centres.

The purple flowers of rhododendron are also showy and bring bright spring colour to the lowland bogs and blanket peat-clad mountain slopes of the west. Unlike the previous two species, however, the beautiful rhododendron is not environmentally harmless. Rhododendron was once native to Ireland, more than 100,000 years ago and long before the interglacial period in which we now live. Today its native range is Turkey and bordering parts of Bulgaria with further populations in the mountains of Lebanon and Syria. It is naturalised in France and Belgium but it has become much more invasive in Ireland and Great Britain as it grows well under temperate moist conditions.

The plant now invading this region is possibly a hybrid between *Rhododendron ponticum* and *Rhododendron catawbiense*. The Worldwide Fund for Nature categorises rhododendron as a serious and widespread invader. It was probably

Sea-buckthorn spreading over sand dunes at the Murlough Nature National Reserve in County Down, from an original planting to stabilise sand around a boat house. The orange berries attract birds.

introduced to numerous sites in the British Isles as an ornamental in the late eighteenth century, but it escaped from cultivation and is now a grave threat to native species as the ground-dwelling plants of the native deciduous woodlands cannot live beneath its shade and leaf litter. Some of the rare mosses of the southwestern oakwoods are much threatened by advancing rhododendron. Perhaps this trait of reducing native biological variety, above all others, separates the invasive aliens from those which are accepted or tolerated.

Rhododendron spreads mainly by seed and bushes can flower from as young as about twelve years. The seeds will germinate under the shade of other trees and are carried by the wind. It will soon colonise many types of soil, including anything from bare mineral soil to rotting wood-rich humus with a clear preference for the drier conditions on cut-over bogs. The dense shade under developing thickets of rhododendron soon reduces the diversity of native species. The plant is resistant to attack by most chemical weed killers and mechanical clearance. Control measures based on its native prey seem unlikely as it has few pests, even in its home range.

Another invasive shrub, albeit more restricted in its range, is the sea-buckthorn (*Hippophaë rhamnoides*). This is one of the plants of disturbed ground that found a place in Ireland soon

The giant hogweed from the Caucasus was brought into gardens for its spectacular architectural shape, but is causing problems where it has spread into areas visited by the public because of the skin lesions its sap can cause.

after the retreat of the ice sheets. It was forced out of Ireland when the forests developed, although it persisted in the east of England. The sea-buckthorn was re-introduced in the nineteenth century to help stabilise sand dunes and has spread aggressively at the expense of existing sand dune vegetation. The sea-buckthorn spreads by underground runners and by the orange fruit dispersed by birds. It forms an impenetrable, spiny thicket about 2m high and its dense summer cover eliminates much of the existing ground vegetation. It does, however, provide both food and shelter for a range of birds and conservation issues involving sea-buckthorn tend to produce a conflict of interest between the ornithologists and the botanists!

At about the same time as rhododendron was introduced to Ireland, the sycamore was first planted. This tree also had its home range in central Europe and it too grows well throughout Ireland and Great Britain. In Ireland it is not considered as serious a pest as rhododendron, but in some places it has taken on some of the less desirable characteristics of an invasive alien. Some years ago considerable effort was put into eradicating it from the sand dune system at Murlough Bay in County Down where the tree cover was threatening the biological diversity of this dune system. The well-known double-winged seeds of the tree germinate readily with seedlings growing strongly in their first season. One could argue that sycamore is acceptable when in its place but it must be recognised that it has a potential environmental danger if left uncontrolled.

Weeds and aliens are not restricted to particular families of plants but two infesting gardens and river banks throughout Ireland and Great Britain belong to the umbellifer family. This family contains many species which are the ancestors of valuable food and flavouring plants like carrot and parsley or the source of famous ancient poisons like hemlock. Most of the members of the family have flat flower heads called umbels and some are tall and decorative. Probably the two least popular members

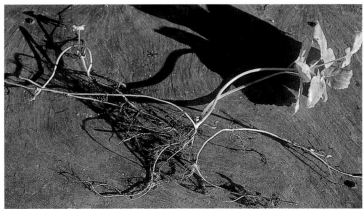

Ground elder or Bishop's weed, in the same family as the giant hogweed, is neither spectacular nor dangerous – just one of the most difficult of all weeds to eradicate as the long white rhizomes travel long distances.

of the family growing in Ireland today are giant hogweed (*Heracleum mantegazzianum*) and ground elder (*Aegopodium podagraria*).

The giant hogweed is a native of the Caucasus and was probably introduced to Ireland from Great Britain at the end of the nineteenth century as a species for the wild gardens so popular at that time. This plant will not be confused with the smaller native hogweed as the giant hogweed is very much larger in all its parts although hybrids between the two species have been found. It is possibly the most massive herbaceous perennial growing under semi-natural conditions in Ireland today. When grown beside water it is indeed a most imposing plant and gives little bother until it comes in contact with human skin. The plant's sap sensitises the skin to sunlight and soon large, painful blisters result. The plant seeds prolifically and the seeds will drift in rivers and streams, taking root on the moist river banks or any other suitable waste ground.

A few years ago the plant was spreading along the River Lagan just beyond suburban Belfast where

Gunnera spreading onto blanket bog in the wet and mild areas of the west coast of Ireland.

undoubtedly it posed a threat to human health. It has now been brought under control but the occasional plant remaining adds a sinister majesty to the banks of the slowly-flowing river. It should be noted that giant hogweed is not unique amongst the umbellifers growing in Ireland in causing skin problems as others like the native hogweed can do the same.

Ground elder is a native woodland plant in most of Europe and temperate Asia but in Ireland and Great Britain, it is the bane of many gardeners' lives. The plant was well known as a medicinal or culinary herb in England during the Middle Ages and fossil pollen evidence suggests it may have arrived first in Roman times, but again, its Irish history is poorly recorded.

It may come into a garden as an unwitting gift from a friend who gives a clump of a choice herbaceous perennial in the depths of whose roots there is a tiny scrap of ground elder's underground stem. This will flourish whether or not the choice perennial does and can spread to cover square metres of previously well-tilled garden soil in a single season. As a ground-cover plant it is unequalled but it seems intent on covering every part of the garden. In this way ground elder has earned itself the double award of being simultaneously an alien and a weed.

If giant hogweed is indeed the heavyweight of the perennials currently growing wild in Ireland, then gunnera (*Gunnera tinctoria*) must be a close second. Like fuchsia, it comes from south and central America and has found a new home in the moist temperate climate and peaty boglands of the western Irish coasts.

It spreads by seed and exhibits one of the strongest characteristics of the successful invasive alien because its seeds can be carried far from the parent plant by birds. Gunnera grows in bog cuttings in many places along the western coast and is thriving on Achill Island and Clare Island off the Mayo coast. Some few years ago plants of gunnera were seen high up on the cliffs at Dookinella on Achill Island, doubtless having grown from a seed lodged in a damp peaty crack in the rock face. The plant is well-suited to the nutrient-poor conditions of Irish cut-over bogs and thin blanket peats because it has the ability to make use of nitrogen from the air, with the assistance of nitrogen-fixing micro-organisms, to form the nitrate nutrient essential for plant growth. Left to itself it may alter the nutrient status of bogland and thus adversely affect the native bog plants which are adapted to living under nitrogen-poor conditions.

Gunnera joins rhododendron and fuchsia as a featured plant in Irish postcards. One popular card shows a picture of a medieval Irish towerhouse with a great sward of bright green gunnera leaves in the foreground! As though our 40 shades of native green were not enough, they have been upstaged by the dramatic newcomers.

The coastal regions are not remote from invasion and in one case a plant purposely introduced to improve a habitat has taken on the role of yet another invasive alien. The cord-grass is wonderfully effective in binding estuarine and coastal mud flats and was therefore popular in the early years of the twentieth century when land was being reclaimed from the sea.

Today the plant has spread round much of the Irish coast but is now being

Cord-grass, a highly competitive hybrid grass, that grows in estuaries and salt marshes, often eliminating all of the existing native vegetation.

Japanese knotweed stems will reach 2m high and will push through concrete and tarmac.

dug out of salt-marshes and mud flats where its vigorous growth would soon out-compete that of other species. Chemical removal of cord-grass from part of the Strangford Lough coastline during the 1980s resulted in what became the longest and most expensive civil court case in Northern Ireland's legal history at that time.

Japanese knotweed (*Reynoutria japonica*, formerly *Polygonum cuspidatum* and also known as *Fallopia japonica*) is also a costly invader to thwart. This tall-stemmed plant with its

Japanese knotweed finds cracks in a city terrace house garden.

New Zealand flax as a hedging plant in the west of Ireland.

fresh green heart-shaped leaves is invading many areas of managed forest and waste ground. It is resistant to most of the commonly-used weed-killers and thrives on any attempt to dig it out. Like the giant hogweed and gunnera, it too was a garden plant which broke out and what garden value it once had has been set aside in the effort to control it. The even larger giant knotweed (*Reynoutria sachalinensis*) is less common than the Japanese knotweed but is fairly widely distributed in Ireland.

Because the spread of aliens world-wide gives great cause for concern, plant scientists have tried to develop mathematical models to predict if an introduced plant is likely to become an invasive alien. So far no model has proved a reliable predictor as the mechanisms influencing invasion are so complex. It is worth noting that though Ireland hosts a number of aliens, some of our most attractive native species are someone else's headache. For example, the hawthorn and whin seen in so many Irish hedges are invasive aliens in New Zealand and the common Irish grasses, cocks-foot and sweet vernal-grass, are considered invasive in Hawaii.

It would be premature to try to predict if the altered germplasm from genetically-engineered crops will enter the gene pool and make weeds and aliens stronger and more resistant to management or eradication than ever before. Our experience with such apparently harmless plants as rhododendron and gunnera suggests we should be cautious.

The invasive alien whin growing with the native New Zealand flax on the west coast of South Island, New Zealand.

9 CONSERVATION AND THE FUTURE

The future of individual species, habitats and whole ecosystems in Ireland is in a state of flux as we write. Political and economic changes are affecting attitudes to the landscape and to conservation at the same time as the effects of global warming start to change the climate system under which our present landscape has evolved.

Let us look at the global warming issue first. Whatever may be the theoretical arguments surrounding the global warming issue, the Irish climate is changing now at a quite rapid rate. The last decade of the twentieth century was the warmest in the last 1,000 years and the effects of this are already apparent in the environment.

The climate 'flip' scenario

While discussing the effects of global climate change, mention should be made of the predictions of some climatologists of a possible climate 'flip' such as happened at the end of the last glaciation. At that time, fresh water from melting glacial ice disrupted the normal sea currents of the North Atlantic, bringing Arctic water to Irish coasts. Some predict that a rise in global temperatures will melt sufficient Arctic ice to, once again, switch off the warm currents to our coasts. This would have the effect of lowering winter temperatures by as much as 30°C. This would fundamentally change many habitats, eliminate many species of both plants and animals – to say nothing of what it would do to agriculture.

These rapid changes are not far in the future, but are predicted for the next 30 to 50 years. Both the fossil record and recent climatic observations make it clear that major changes *will* happen and that these changes *will* affect Ireland's wildlife and agriculture.

What effects can be seen already and what may reasonably be predicted? The responses will vary with habitat. Based on the past behaviour of the habitats, the least impact may be expected on woodland communities, a rather greater impact on grasslands and the greatest impact on coastal and wetland habitats.

Political pressure, deriving from the realisation that global warming is happening, will increase the demand for carbon-neutral technologies such as wind power. The impact of large-scale use of wind power in Ireland is yet to be assessed.

Woodlands

The fossil record suggests that mature woodland has considerable resistance to change and an ability to survive short-term climate fluctuations. Because the trees in woodland are long-lived, any short-term fluctuations in seed production or seedling survival will not affect the overall forest composition. Where a longer-term climate shift occurs, as is now predicted, it would be reasonable to expect a change in the composition of woodland with more drought-resistant species being favoured. This is probably of little significance in comparison with the woodland composition changes brought about by the introduction of alien trees such as sycamore.

Azolla, a water-fern from tropical America has spread northwards in Ireland over the last few decades.

Bogs and wetlands

Already there are signs of the drying of bog surfaces all over Ireland, with greater decay in the upper few centimetres of raised bogs than in peats of any time in the last 4,000 years. The nearest parallel to this is the drying of bogs and the colonisation by pine in the mid-post glacial (see Chapter 5). This trend is, of course, superimposed on the drying of bogs through drainage and peat harvesting. Drying of blanket bogs will also exacerbate the break-up and erosion of upland peats, brought about by overgrazing and mechanical peat harvesting.

It may be a few years yet before water chestnut (*Trapa natans*) clogs the waterways and hydro-electric schemes of the Shannon as this weed has little frost tolerance. Other aquatics, however, are already making an impact. The aquatic water-fern (*Azolla filiculoides*), a native of tropical America, is spreading in Ireland. It was known as far north as Wicklow in the 1950s, but has recently been found in a number of lakes in the north of Ireland including the Glastry Brick Works Nature Reserve, in County Down where another recently arrived alien, *Crassula helmsii*, is also spreading.

Sea shore

The biggest threat to coastal communities is a rise in sea level. A few years ago there were scare stories of sea level rises of many metres brought about by the melting of Arctic and Antarctic ice. This is now thought to be unlikely, but there will still be a sea level rise due to expansion of the ocean water as it warms. This is likely to increase global

Crassula helmsii, a native of Australia and New Zealand, was sold to gardeners for oxygenating ponds. It has now been found in at least three locations in Ireland and appears to be spreading.

sea levels by some 45cm in the next 50 years, thus having a detrimental effect on salt marshes which in a natural environment could migrate inland as the sea level rose. In modern Ireland this would be prevented by coastal roads and flood defences.

Sand dunes may also be affected both by a rise in sea level and a predicted increase in storminess. The very nature of sand dune ecosystems depends on a degree of instability opening up new areas of fresh sand and on the wind creating new dunes. The sand dunes may change but the plants and habitats will probably survive.

Weeds and aliens

There are parallels between the present rising global temperatures and times of rapid temperature rise at the end of the last glaciation. At this time competitive and invasive plants from further south ousted the native Arctic flora of Ireland and became the new native plants of this island.

One of the most obvious effects of recent climate change in Ireland has been the milder winters. Little more than a century ago the replenishment of the ice houses of the great country houses of Ireland relied on the regular freezing of lakes. This has not happened since the 1960s. On a shorter time scale, gardeners all over Ireland report the survival of tender plants that have been impossible to grow out-of-doors until the last two decades. This gives us another clue to

likely habitat impacts of future climate change. Plants such as gunnera are sensitive to winter freezing and the current spread on the west coast is surely facilitated by recent warm winters. We can expect plants like this to expand their range at the expense of less competitive but frost-hardy native species.

Politics, Economics and Conservation

In the light of these predicted climatic changes how should we view conservation issues? If the external factors controlling the environment in Ireland are changing, is it appropriate to try to preserve modern environments?

Nature conservation is not about returning areas to their 'natural state' – there is only one natural state in most of Ireland and that is a dense mixed forest. If all existing Irish environments are human influenced, if not actually human made, then this poses a fundamental question. Why protect or conserve such habitats? Would it not be better to encourage the wholesale stripping of blanket peat so that the wind-swept mountains could be returned to forest – the 'natural' environment of Ireland's uplands? What about a strategy for grasslands? Should selected grasslands be conserved by keeping out all people and domestic animals and allow the natural process of succession to replace the grassland with wet fen or dry-land forest? What really is the aim of conservation? Is it just a middle-class ideal of trying to retain a pretty landscape for picnics or for walking the dog? Is it a biologist's ideal of retaining biological diversity at all costs – turning the landscape into a huge botanic gardens and zoo? Or is it, in the end, just a financial decision based on the preservation of habitats that have income potential for tourism?

The reality of conservation in Ireland at the present time lies somewhere between the pretty flower ideal and the biologist's biodiversity ideal. The tasks facing conservationists in Ireland are so severe that there is little opportunity for a long-term view of conservation or of realisation that natural habitats evolve. Most conservation seeks to pickle habitats at a particular point in their evolution. In reality the only Irish habitat that is likely to remain stable without intervention is woodland and here the species composition of the end product may not be at all what the present generation of conservationists would consider acceptable. A sycamore/eucalyptus forest with an understorey of rhododendron might develop naturally and become stable, but would it be considered desirable?

Conservation policy in Ireland is now becoming increasingly influenced by policy decisions made in the European Union. These directives are slow to filter down to the local level where action is possible, but will in time provide greater protection for a least a small number of key sites.

This legislative approach to conservation will not protect the little patches of woodland in field corners, the grassland on a railway embankment, or the plants in a disused quarry. Here it is the attitude of the general public that needs to change so that these little squares in the patchwork of Ireland are given the care they deserve.

Set against the increasing conservation legislation and improvements in public awareness are the huge pressure that an increasing population make for housing, roads, airports and fuel. New pressures will arise as a consequence of global warming issues. Now that the reality of global warming is dawning on politicians, schemes to reduce the use of fossil fuel will increase. The production of biomass for fuel using willow coppice is under trial in several places in Ireland. This is a 'carbon-neutral' fuel. This means that the willow absorbs as much carbon dioxide from the atmosphere as it gives out when the fuel is burned. To make a realistic contribution to the energy requirements of the island, large areas would have to be planted. As the willow plantations would be in wetland habitats the conservation implications are serious. Another source of energy under active development in Ireland is wind power. We may expect to see extensive areas of the uplands and west coast covered by wind farms. The implications of this for conservation have yet to be assessed.

The combination of increasing population and the unknowns of global warming may suggest a grim future for the flora and fauna of Ireland, but the past provides models which suggest otherwise. The survival of the Arctic and Alpine flora of the Burren for 10,000 years against the enormous pressure of woodland advance is remarkable. No less remarkable is the development of species rich grassland on motorways and railway embankments just as the pasture grassland dwindles due to changing agricultural practices. In the future the land under wind farms may become another new habitat protected from people-pressure and there is no doubt that climate change will create new habitats just as surely as it will destroy some old ones. The varied landscape and geology of Ireland ensure that it will always have a plant life of great diversity – even if not as we would recognise it.

BIBLIOGRAPHY

Aalen, F.H.A., Whelan, K. and Stout, M. 1997. *Atlas of the rural Irish landscape.* Cork University Press, Cork.

Beesley, S and Wilde, J. 1997. *Urban flora of Belfast.* The Institute of Irish Studies, Queen's University Belfast, Belfast.

Carruthers, T. 1998. *Kerry: a natural history.* The Collins Press, Cork.

Clapham, A.R., Tutin, T.G. and Moore, D.M. 1987. *Flora of the British Isles.* 3rd edition. Cambridge University Press, Cambridge.

Curtis, T.G.F. and McGough, H.N 1988. *The Irish red data book: 1 Vascular Plants.* Wildlife Service, Office of Public Works, Dublin.

D'Arcy, G. 1992. *The natural history of the Burren.* Immel Publishing, London.

Foss, P.J. (Ed.) 1991. *Irish peatlands, the critical decade.* Irish Peatland Conservation Council, Dublin

Garrard, I. and Streeter, D. 1993. *The wild flowers of the British Isles.* Midsummer Books, London.

Hackney, P. 1992. *Stewart and Corry's flora of the North-East of Ireland.* (3rd Edition). The Institute of Irish Studies, Belfast.

Harron, J. 1986. *Flora of Lough Neagh.* Irish Naturalists' Journal, Belfast.

Heery, Stephen 1993. *The Shannon floodlands: a natural history of the Shannon callows.* Tír Eolas, Newtownlynch.

Jeffrey, D.W., Jones, M.B. and McAdam, J.H. 1995. *Irish grasslands: their biology and management.* Royal Irish Academy, Dublin.

Jermy, A.C., Chater, A.O. and David, R.W. 1982. *Sedges of the British Isles.* BSBI Handbook No 1. Botanical Society of the British Isles, London.

Merryweather, J. and Hill, M. 1992. *The fern guide: an introductory guide to the ferns, clubmosses, quillworts and horsetails of the British Isles.* Field Studies 8 (1992), 101-188.

Mitchell, F. and Ryan, M. 1997. *Reading the Irish landscape.* Town House, Dublin.

Nelson, E.C. and Walsh, W. 1991. *The Burren: a companion to the wild flowers of an Irish limestone wilderness.* Boethius Press, Kilkenny.

O'Connell, J.W. and Korff, A. (Eds) 1991. *The book of the Burren.* Tír Eolas, Newtownlynch.

O'Connell, M. 1994. *Connemara: vegetation and land use since the last ice age.* The Office of Public Works, Dublin.

Pilcher, J.R. and Mac an tSaoir, S. (Eds) 1995. *Wood, trees and forests in Ireland*. Royal Irish Academy, Dublin.

Praeger, R.L. 1937 *The way that I went*. Reprinted by The Collins Press, Cork, 1997.

Scannell, M.J.P. and Synnott, D.M. 1987. *Census catalogue of Ireland*, 2nd edition. Stationery Office, Dublin.

Steer, M. (Ed.) 1991. *Irish Rivers: biology and management*. Royal Irish Academy, Dublin.

Sweeney, J. (Ed.) 1997. *Global change and the Irish Environment*. Royal Irish Academy, Dublin.

Tutin, T.G. 1980. *Umbellifers of the British Isles*. BSBI Handbook No 2. Botanical Society of the British Isles, London.

Webb, D.A., Parnell, J. and Doogue, D. 1996. *An Irish Flora*. Dundalgan Press, Dundalk.

Whilde, T. 1994. *The natural history of Connemara*. Immel Publishing, London.

PLANT INDEX